In the Paradise of Krishna

IN THE PARADISE OF KRISHNA

Hindu and Christian Seekers

by KLAUS KLOSTERMAIER

W The Westminster Press · Philadelphia

© SCM Press Ltd 1969

Translated by Antonia Fonseca from the German
published by Verlag Jakob Hegner in Cologne

Published in Great Britain under the title
Hindu and Christian in Vrindaban

ISBN 0-664-24904-3
LIBRARY OF CONGRESS CATALOG CARD No. 76-128022

PUBLISHED BY THE WESTMINSTER PRESS ®
PHILADELPHIA, PENNSYLVANIA

PRINTED IN THE UNITED STATES OF AMERICA

Contents

TO MY MOTHER

Introduction

by John V Taylor

I have never been to Vrindaban. But the little town with the sweetly musical name is well known throughout India as the place where Lord Krishna romped with the milkmaids and fell in love with Radha. The epic of their passion has become an allegory of divine love, and it is the longing for God which sends pilgrims in their hundreds of thousands back to the little town year after year. No more appropriate place could have been chosen for Klaus Klostermaier's home. For he came there as a young man of twenty-nine in love with love, and he gave himself to this quest with the extravagant endurance that only India knows.

It was a far cry from the home in Munich and the boyhood nightmares of the bombing raids. The libraries of philosophy and ethnology in Vienna and Rome seemed remote and unreal, as he says, in the furnace of a crowded back street during the months before the monsoon. What held him there when other missionaries escaped to the hills was the spell of fascination – the fascination of people he was learning to know, the fascination of their so different experience of life and of the Spirit, the fascination, above all, of the knowledge of Christ.

The pursuit is an intellectual one. Following in the steps of the great Roberto de Nobili, this member of the Order of the Divine Word brings to his devotion to India the meticulous training of a philosopher and theologian. Yet his approach is that of a friendship rather than of scholarship, and his search for understanding is both humble and human. This is what is so often missing in our so-called inter-religious dialogue. Too often this is set up as an encounter of representatives in a contest of comparisons or, worse still, a contest of courtesies. And those who argue the theoretical pros and cons of dialogue as a missionary method seem unable to imagine that the adherents of different faiths can meet simply as friends. But unless it grows out of the gentle delving and slow maturing of friendship, dialogue is only an exercise in indifference, the very antithesis of love.

The real thing does not happen mainly in the study or the classroom, but in the home and the bazaar, on the pilgrimage and in the temple. It is just as interested in the other man's unbelief as in his belief, in what he regards as secular as in what he regards as sacred. So a great deal of the value of this exquisite book lies in its uncomplicated delight in people and the places they live in. It is a long time since I have enjoyed such a gallery of rogues and saints. And, after all, it is rogues and saints, not Christianity or Hinduism, that are the object of a truly religious concern. Whenever I come across any pundits debating the good or ill of dialogue I shall in future ask them whether they have read this book.

But, naturally, as the author meditates on the significance of the things that friendships have taught him he is led into the profoundest questions concerning his own faith and philosophy. It is an enormous adventure to try to follow his thought as it presses on into the new meanings which he finds in the Lord Jesus. For always it is the love for Christ which constrains him, identified with, yet surpassing, his love for the mind of India. And such is the courage of his exploration that even faith itself is at risk for the sake of that further discovery of the length and breadth, the depth and height, of the love of Christ which beckons him on.

That great and scholarly gentleman, Dr Zakir Hussain, the late President of India, was asked shortly before his death what it was that the Republic still needed most of all from the Western nations. Without a moment's hesitation he replied, 'Understanding'. He would have been grateful for this book.

Sacred Vrindaban

For two years I have lived in Vrindaban, one of the most popular Hindu places of pilgrimage in Northern India. Situated on the Yamuna, forty miles north of Agra, Brajbhumi, the area around Mathura, represents the 'body of Krishna' for the Krishnabhaktas – divine in an immediate and tangible sense. Mathura has been revered for more than two thousand years as the birthplace of Krishna. Romantic Vrindaban, about ten miles up-river, is the place of the Krishnalila, the love-play of Krishna with the gopis, the milkmaids. Radha is his favourite gopi; present-day bhaktas regard her as the earthly incarnation of the consort of God. Vrindaban is Krishna's paradise; only in Vrindaban can the highest degree of prema-bhakti be attained, as the gopis possessed it. The everlasting bodily presence of Krishna is strictly divided among the separate villages of Brajbhumi district. An elderly gentleman, who accosted me in the market-place to hold an impromptu speech on bhakti for my benefit, explained to me that 'in Vrindaban, he who has eyes to see can observe Krishna and Radha at their love-play even today'.

Every year, an average of over two million pilgrims come here. Quite an upheaval for a town of hardly 40,000 inhabitants. Vrindaban has a number of big temples and countless small ones. The people here maintain that 'Vrindaban has seven thousand temples'. I am often asked whether I did not also feel the special divinity of the place, the presence of Krishna manifest, as it is for a bhakta, in so many places. One of my friends would only call me Krishnakumar and he would urge me constantly to give myself up to Krishna. 'Radhe Shyam' is the greeting of the people here; I should do the same, they say, thus honouring those whose praise is sung by thousands day and night here in Vrindaban. Vrindaban is the shrine of Krishna-love.

An elderly Bengali Vaishnava monk, inspired by the large theological colleges he had seen on his missionary tours of Europe and America, had the idea of erecting a Vaishnava theological college in the holy place of Krishna. He was convinced of his own religion, but generous enough to include, in his planning, professorial chairs for various non-Hindu religions, to be occupied by representatives of those religions.

After many a complicated series of events, it so happened that I took over the 'St Peter's Chair for Christian Philosophy' there, in order to start, in addition to my own research and study of various aspects of Hinduism, a department of 'Christianity' in the Vaishnava college. Friends at home helped to get up a small library with the essential Christian literature and to give a scholarship to an Indian Christian layman, enabling him to graduate there with a thesis on comparative religious study. The Indian bishops' conference gave its blessing.

In the course of two years, many things happened in Vrindaban, and this little book is not intended to be a chronological register of the days and weeks spent there. It is meant to relate experiences that seem to me typical – thoughts that occupied my mind for a long time, impressions that it seems worthwhile to relate to others. Friends urged me to publish something of what I had written down purely for private purposes, since the 'experiment in Sacred Vrindaban' was not altogether a common one and because the insights I gained there through daily, intimate contact with Hindus might also have some meaning for the 'dialogue'. These are personal experiences and personal reflections and I do not want to generalize from what I have experienced and what I have thought. To those who have no opportunity of entering into 'dialogue' with followers of other religions it may give a little insight into the reality of inward and outward dialogue with Hinduism – also into the painful and slow process of learning to think afresh and to give up cherished prejudices or ingrained ways of thinking. This is what happens to the thoughts of a man who gives himself up to the dialogue in the setting of another religion.

Life in Vrindaban is typical of that in an orthodox Hindu town, still living largely in and by Hinduism. Twice a day, a narrow-gauge train chugs the ten miles from Mathura to Vrindaban. Arrival and departure times are always approximate; no one in Vrindaban is in a hurry. The saffron-coloured robes of sadhus abound even in the train. No sooner do the first temple towers of Vrindaban come into sight than the devout women pilgrims break into a chorus of rapturous praise for Krishna. The same happens in the bus, which runs 'frequently'. So, too, in the tongas, those fleet little horse-carriages, still the main transport of pilgrims. During times of major pilgrimages, camel buses move on Vrindaban: large, cage-like wagons, double-decked and with room for about twenty-five passengers; speed, two miles per hour. The camels pulling the wagons pretend to have nothing whatsoever to do with the people they are pulling. The more affluent are transported speedily and almost always safely in cycle-rickshaws. The cycle-rickshaws wind their way through herds of cattle, crowds of people and drainpipe-narrow streets. Past large and small temples, past new houses and ruins, past small open stalls, most of them selling devotional items, and past small artisan shops. The general impression is not unfriendly, and the town is cleaner than most. Many rich people build themselves country residences for their retirement, surrounded by large parks with beautiful trees. There are no factories, no large administrative offices, no resident Europeans, no missions. The people are Hindu in body and soul – in thought, feeling and speech. They are their natural selves. The atmosphere is filled with the drone of drums, the tinkling of bells and the incessant, chorus-like invocations of Krishna and Radha: in the temples, in the houses, on the streets, in the fields. Everything and everybody sings the praises of the divine couple. There are several thousand devout widows in Vrindaban from all corners of India. They sing, in shifts, the praises of Krishna and Radha in the temples and are rewarded with a simple meal and some pocket-money. Family planning is as yet restricted to a small government centre; the streets abound with jolly children in high spirits and of all age groups. Just like their mothers, little five-year-old girls carry their baby-brothers on their hips, taking them to the children's meeting grounds. Their games are the games of children all over the world – large signs and rectangles are drawn on the road with chalk and the children hop about them in a particular way; one jumps over a swinging rope, another plays with marbles and does target practice with bits of wood. Nobody finds the children disturbing, no one gets annoyed if they lay claim to a portion of the road – nobody resents the children for being what they are . . .

The most interesting and striking feature of Vrindaban is without doubt the sadhus. Most of these monks are Vaish-navas; they are recognized by means of their characteristic tilak, the coloured sign on their forehead. Many of them always carry a rosary of 108 tulsi beads, letting it glide through their fingers, calling on God incessantly. But other groups also have their representatives. Vrindaban resembles a monks'

4

camp, especially during the time of caturmas, the four-month-long rainy period, for which sadhus are allowed to remain in one place. Long queues of sadhus can be seen daily in the kshetras, those places set up by the wealthy for the distribution of food to holy men. Most of these wear the saffron-coloured sadhu robes. Orthodox Vaishnavas don white robes, draping them around their bodies in picturesque folds. Others replace clothing with some ash or clay paint. Some simply dig a hole in the sand and erect a wind-shield made of reeds, others live in a simple room sparsely furnished with a few musical instruments, a dozen books. Many live in groups in the extensive temple compounds and ashramas. There is something for every taste; the only thing is that one must not act out of character. Some have vowed themselves to silence, speaking for a mere ten minutes after sundown, and then only bare essentials; others lead as good a life as bad times and good people permit. Some appear ragged and neglected; others tidy and well-groomed. Some have studied various subjects for years; others are illiterate. Some were simply brought up to be sadhus and, as children, had to beg for their guru; others retire out of a genuine inner vocation. Some are kind and serene and consider all men their brothers and sisters; others are hard and fanatic and fight everything that does not follow their own sectional dogma to the letter. Very recently, some sadhus have come together in sevashramas to do 'social work'. In Vrindaban, there are also several goshalas – old-age homes for cows: wealthy, orthodox business people donate a large piece of land, have good stables built, engage people and buy good fodder in order to sweeten the last few years of 'mother cow'. It is difficult to discern how much of this is piety and how much politics, what part business sense plays and what part superstition. Even among sadhus who are supposed to give up all social ties, there are more and more politicians, who stand for election and go on tour. Even the swami in whose institute I worked had been a parliamentary candidate under the flag of the Ram Rajya Parishad – the 'Kingdom of God' party founded by another swami.

Life is fairly simple in Vrindaban; there are no very rich people and there is no gross poverty; all have the basic essentials. As in all places of pilgrimage, there are many lepers, many beggars knowing that the pious are more likely to distribute alms here than elsewhere.

Vrindaban would be less interesting without its animal world. We are all complete vegetarians here: no meat the whole year round, no fish, no eggs, no onions, no garlic. Eating prescriptions are an essential part of Vaishnavism: only the 'pure' nourishment as prescribed in their religion may be taken. Animals in Vrindaban do not have to fear men. Braj has been famous for its wealth of cattle since antiquity. There are many representations of the 'divine cowherd' Krishna, playing on his silver flute and dancing in front of an immense herd of exquisitely pretty white cows. Towards sundown, it is still a picturesque sight to watch the boys and girls in the midst of their flocks of cows, buffaloes, goats and sheep, seemingly afloat on a cloud of fine dust before a golden red sky, returning to town from the lowlands near the river. The boys play old, simple, often lilting melodies on their five-tone bamboo flutes, and the girls mark the time with their anklets, tinkling at every step.

The holy cows and steers have only Krishna as their lord; they are free of human masters and seem conscious of their dignity. Nobody can force them to labour. Actually, the greengrocer at whose stall a cow thinks of satisfying her appetite should deem himself honoured by such attention; but normally he will try to satisfy his sensibilities as well as his business sense by diverting the animal's attention with some scraps. The children often have their fun irritating and rousing one of the huge black bulls who might be somewhat enfeebled with old age and weak on his legs. Motherly, lonely old women buy a few extra leaves of vegetable to feed a holy cow. There are dogs in Vrindaban – countless and defying description, in all shapes and colours, bowlegged in front and paralysed behind, mangy and scurfy, small ones, large ones, fat ones, skinny ones – they lie everywhere, bark always, annoy everyone. It disturbs nobody. At night, the jackals come into town. Their malicious laughter mingles with the angry howling of the dogs and the offended shrieking of the peacocks – a polyphonous and impressive serenade.

There is nothing more beautiful than the many peacocks strutting around the gardens and fields, adorning walls and trees. Even here, they look a little exotic. In few places is the feathered world as diverse as it is here. Hundreds of birds of prey circle for hours in convergent spirals in the sun-drenched midday sky. Wherever there is a carcass dozens of pugnacious vultures with ugly, long, naked red necks congregate within minutes. Countless waterfowl populate the meadows near the Yamuna; some seem to consist merely of infinitely long, thin legs, others of broad yellow bills. Rose-hued flamingoes stalk through the shallow water. Cackling dark-brown wild ducks fly low over the fields in formation. Thousands of bright-green parrots with brilliant red beaks play and shriek in the trees; delicate, tiny birds, golden-coloured and with a metallic glimmer whirr from blossom to blossom. Gaily mottled hoopoes knock on the shutters; cheekily talkative minahs bustle around. Cooing, calling and fighting doves nest everywhere – and above all, sly and patient, the ubiquitous crows. No one harms the animals, and so they are not shy. Ever new and surprising shapes and colour compositions can be discovered, fantastic creatures, as if they had come from the studio of a surrealist artist.

7

The insects deserve special appreciation. During the dry season, few are seen. Outdoors it is too hot for them, and indoors the ever-present lizards check their population. But in the rainy season these vermin-destroyers, the lizards, only select the juiciest bits. Unchecked, the remaining millions of insects proceed to attack poor humanity which is no longer capable of defending itself against the unnumbered creeping, crawling, jumping enemy, against the little black and grey and green and brown cuirasses, against the long and short daggers, against the white, red and black wings, against the tiny ones and the cigar-length ones, against the staunch and well-known ones and against the most bizarre new discoveries. This insect army tweaks and stings, it whirrs and buzzes, it jumps and twangs, it stinks and spreads its fragrance . . .

As cheeky as street-boys are the monkeys, quick and nimble, always bent on annoying somebody. Shoes, hats, scarves and turbans are the favourite toys of these inhabitants of Vrindaban. Even they are under divine protection, and more than one temple is dedicated to their king, who helped Rama bring Sita back from Lanka.

Love for animals passes all bounds: dignified old gentlemen are seen to keep milk and wheat ready for the rats of the house – rats are the 'companions' of the god Ganesha, the patron of businessmen and scholars. Men and animals belong together here in Vrindaban; they tease and fight each other and yet get on quite well together.

Night and day, the praises of Krishna and Radha are sung and played in Vrindaban. Everywhere, their picture hangs, everywhere their statues stand, everywhere there is a tree, a stone, a temple, a square connected with a particular incident in the life of Krishna. On many an evening, there are performances of the Ras-Lila in various squares in town, performed by colourfully decked out boys in front of an ever-ecstatic public.

In the temples it happens again and again that serious-minded men go into a trance and see Radha in every woman, Krishna in every man, prostrate themselves in front of everybody and kiss every passer-by's feet. During the major feasts, an immense wave of feeling and emotion sweeps the whole town, and one even begins to wonder whether it may not indeed be true that Krishna and Radha have returned to earth in order to enchant the human race with their love-play.

Pilgrimage is a basic exercise in Hindu religion. Each place has its own attraction: here a man may get rid of his sins, there he finds 'deliverance'. But only in Vrindaban is it possible to achieve gopi-bhakti, the highest form of love for Krishna. Many people cover long distances each year to come to Vrindaban. Even ministers and directors of large factories come in their cars to visit their gurus, to throw themselves into the dust in front of them and to kiss their feet. Incurably ill people come here in the hope of finding a cure, married couples wishing for children, students afraid of failing an exam. Business people continuously courting Lakshmi's favours, guilt-ridden men, everyone of them brings a request to the temple. Lights are lit in honour of God, strongly fragrant joss sticks are burnt, stones and sculptures are touched, kissed, sprinkled with water and blossoms, hung with garlands.

The major Hindu feasts are celebrated all over India, but quite naturally with special pomp in the places of pilgrimage. The Hindu calendar is still a moon calendar; the dates of the feasts are determined by the position of the moon. Therein lies a great deal of their fascination. The Indian moon is not the pale street lantern of Northern Europe, she is a nocturnal sun – large and beautiful and cool, a great magician changing the poorest landscape into a fairy garden. Nobody can resist this transformation; under the Indian moon even the prosaic European soon ceases to have difficulty in believing in Radha and Krishna and in the games of the gopis, especially since he sees them played again and again by the local boys and girls. Janmashtami, Krishna's birthday, is the main feast in Vrindaban. It is celebrated with immense pomp and a gathering of masses of people from all over India. Radhashtami, Radha's birthday, is celebrated with equal brilliance by the Radhavallabhis, with nocturnal processions and boys playing on silver flutes.

Shivaratri has a special character in a town completely dedicated to Krishna, where it is a sin to think of a god who might be greater than Krishna. Throughout the night, the villagers come on their ox- and horsecarts, loud and unruly, singing the praises of the god whose generative powers are unfathomable. Throughout the day, a stream of people flows into the town. Early in the morning, the most solemn service takes place: the shivalingam, a phallic symbol, is bathed in water brought by special bearers from the Ganges in Soronj, a hundred miles away. It is compulsory to remove one's shoes outside, far outside; the queues of the devout are very long. Hawkers sell cheap, vividly coloured clay figures which the villagers take home with them as toys for their children. At the entrance to the temple stands a figure with a demon's grimace – Shiva's bodyguard. Then come the figures of Krishna and Radha, of Hanuman and Nandi, Shiva's bull. In the temple proper there are no sculptures, only a huge black basalt lingam resting on a large representation of a womb. People press from all sides – pouring water and milk on to the lingam, scattering flowers on it, rubbing it ardently with their right hand. Then they circumambulate the lingam.

Why do these Krishna-bhaktas venerate Shiva? Near the Shiva temple there is a place surrounded by a high wall with a tall tree in the centre. Here Krishna used to meet the gopis to delight in dancing. Only girls were allowed there. But Shiva was curious – he changed himself into a young girl and slipped through the gate. His light-coloured skin giving him away, he had to admit his trickery. But Krishna had mercy on him and assured him that, henceforward, no one could approach Krishna without first having honoured Shiva. These scenes are depicted on the inside wall by unsophisticated naïve paintings.

A big rathmela is celebrated in Vrindaban, just as in Puri and other places. At the beginning of the hot season, the likeness of Vishnu, the Lord of Ranganji Mandir, is brought in solemn procession to his summer residence, in a richly ornamented wagon as large as a house and accompanied by thousands of people. For this occasion, special trains are run from Delhi, and special long-distance buses. For days before the feast, the villagers camp on the roadside, where they bake their bread, cook their vegetables and await the great day.

Krishna-Jhula during the rainy season is another interesting feast: swings are fixed everywhere, and figures of Radha and Krishna placed in them. In the old temples there are solid silver swings, in one temple even a golden one. Families possess small wooden ones, the delight especially of children. On a certain day in the year, thousands of people congregate in the Bankey Biharji Mandir to wait for midnight, when the swing with the famous image of Radhakrishna is set in motion. Deafeningly shrill cries and calls mark the moment when the highest officiating brahmin unveils the idol and pushes the swing. Priests sprinkle water, in which the image had previously been bathed, on the crowd.

Parikrama, the circumambulation of the whole town, is a very popular custom in Vrindaban, and there is hardly a pilgrim who would miss it. Parikrama is especially meritorious on Ekadashi, the eleventh of the moon halves. In order to attain the fruits of a religious action, the most exacting ways of going around the town limits are thought of and done. For many days and nights, an uninterrupted stream of pilgrims walks in single file around Vrindaban.

In Vrindaban, Holi is celebrated for a full week. Little boys are allowed to do anything they please, between sunrise and sundown. Children and grown-ups, cows and dogs are splashed with red colour, with green colour, with ink, with filth from the gutter (which also serves as a public lavatory). Indecorous things are called out to strangers, improper words written on paper and pinned to unsuspecting people's clothing. An especially interesting custom is observed during the last three days: on a long road, thousands of people form a lane. On roofs and ledges, on balconies and verandahs, on window-sills and trees, thousands sit in their holiday garb – a picture so full of life and colour as only the orient can paint. Ten, twenty, fifty, a hundred robust young women clad in colourful saris emerge into the street. They are armed with strong sticks, many of them reinforced with iron. With these, they fly at the defenceless men, at first only playfully choosing some relatives who are allowed to hold a stick for self-defence. Soon the game gets livelier, and more realistic. Wherever a male being can be found, he is beaten hard and long until he flees. Many believe in demonstrating manly courage and endure it surprisingly long – but not as long as the women. The amazons seem to have had some training. The cruel persecution of men in Vrindaban stops only at nightfall. Different countries, different customs. . . . Of course, this scene is only another reminder of Krishna: when Krishna played his flute every evening in the meadows of Vrindaban, inviting the milkmaids to dance with him, the gopas, i.e. the husbands, brothers and fathers of the gopis, would not allow them to run after Krishna. But Krishna has to be obeyed, even at the expense of fathers and brothers and husbands. The gopis broke loose by tricks and violence, following Krishna and his love.

Even in Vrindaban, life is not always without sorrow. The naïve piety, the natural gaiety show flaws and cracks. The disappointment and bitterness of life, suffering and misery, loneliness and illness, death and old age are realities even here, compelling people to probe beyond the surface of a gay, traditionally popular religion into the deeper strata of truth. Here also there is fear and uncertainty, doubting of religious authority and despairing of the gods. It takes some time till one finds, beyond all the exotic colour and uniqueness of expression, the actual problems and even the tragedy. There are many honest and pious people here, but also many who only wish for a fool's paradise, who cannot bear the idea of a demanding God, but only require an idol freely distributing health and wealth. There are many for whom religion means business or politics, many who do not wish to enter the kingdom of God and also try to prevent others from doing so. There are many who speak of love for God and have no love for their neighbour; there are many who impose upon themselves severe renunciation, and there are also many hypocrites.

Parikrama

The night was fabulously beautiful. The full moon in the western sky shone so brightly that it was almost impossible to discern the stars. Crickets chirped gently. The air was filled with a soft singing as if the gandharvas, the heavenly musicians, were practising. The shaggy, thorny shrubs and trees took on the appearance of dancing nymphs. A sweet fragrance wafted from somewhere. The dry grass was softly fanned by the warm breeze. It was four o'clock in the morning and we began our pilgrimage with a view to finishing our round before it became too unbearably hot.

'Hare Krishna!', Dr Govindam called out. He was our guide, a believing bhakta, who had come here immediately after his retirement from higher civil service, wishing to dedicate the rest of his life to the attainment of Krishna-bhakti. There were three of us; besides me another young Hindu by the name of Sanat, a candidate for a doctor's degree who also had some journalistic experience. The previous evening, Dr Govindam had explained to us the basic rules of Parikrama: the whole walk is done barefoot, in single file; if not singing the name of Krishna, one should meditate or speak about him. Only then was punya, the profit of Parikrama, assured.

We were not the first ones. Pilgrims from other parts of the country chose these beautiful moonlit nights for their all-night trek. They sang their bhajans, beating the time with drums and cymbals. The clear and loud voices of the little children and the harsher, deeper ones of the men, the strong voices of the village women and the reserved, soft voices of the genteel ladies – all of them sang the praises of Krishna and Radha and all of them went this way in search of greater love for him, perhaps even to behold him in reality. For even today the great bhaktas of Vrindaban relate how it is possible to discover Krishna peeping archly from behind a tree, dancing his rasa dance with the gopis during especially blessed times, or to meet Radha on a lonely path, enquiring after her lover Krishna.

Soft sand flowed up between our toes. We neither sang nor spoke. The moon shone bright and cool. Soft music flowed through the air. Drums and cymbals sounded from a nearby temple. Morning bhajans had begun. They had been playing and singing all night through – the early morning is one of those special times when the image of a god is venerated and the name of God called out with devotion and strength. 'Ramon Reti' is the name of the tract of land through which we were passing: 'pleasant sands'. We were wading almost knee-deep in it. On top it was cool, deep down it had stored the previous day's warmth.

Dr Govindam broke the silence. 'We ought to try and imagine Krishna as a child, how he played in the sands, building sand castles, how he wallowed in it and threw it at his little friends.' It was not difficult to imagine this. Had we not often observed this game, played by old and young alike, in memory of Krishna? Large trees emerged from the background, banyan trees with hanging air roots as thick as arms. Some of these roots had pierced the strong brick wall of the garden enclosure. A few peacocks, shrieking sleepily, fluttered on to a higher branch. On our right, a small roadside temple in honour of Shiva: a small shrine containing a lingam lit up by a flickering oil-lamp. An almost naked Shaivite monk with long, pinned-up hair sat cross-legged in front of the lingam. Motionless, he stared at the Shivalingam in the fitful bluish light. He might have sat there the whole night – probably many nights. Perhaps years. He wanted to see Shiva. He did not bat an eyelid when Dr Govindam bowed low and greeted him with folded hands. We wandered on through the pleasant sands. How beautiful and how enchanting it was!

Dr Govindam thought it his duty as a bhakta to tell us more about Krishna, his life and work, his miraculous birth and his even more miraculous redemption from the tyrant Kamsa, the marvellous deeds propounded by him when a mere infant: Dr Govindam seems to know a great deal of the Bhagavata Puranas by heart; he recited whole chapters of the poetic Sanskrit texts from memory.

Kamsa, the tyrant of Mathura, who had not been able to kill Krishna immediately after his birth, sent Putana, the she-devil who walked the cities and villages killing little children. She approached Krishna's cradle in the shape of a lovely young woman. She took him into her arms, to nurse him with her poisoned milk. But Krishna, the redeemer of the world, not only drained her of her poison but also of her life, and Putana, the infanticide, fell dead. Krishna had accomplished his first redemptive act. But by the contact with his mouth he had not only delivered the world from Putana; he had also released her from her own evil nature. Whoever comes into contact with Krishna – be it in love or in hate, receiving life or death – is redeemed.

We had left the 'pleasant sands', the ground was firm now. Trees stood on either side. 'It could have been here,' said Dr Govindam, 'that Krishna slew the two demons in the shape of donkeys.' He simply grabbed them by their hind legs and whirled them about in the air before shattering them against a tree trunk. 'Hare Krishna!'

Young Krishna is called 'Krishna Natkhat': Krishna the good-for-nothing. He has played divinely delightful pranks. He and his brother Balarama hung on to the tails of calves, raided the villagers' larders for milk and butter, were up to mischief in the houses. One day, the gopas told Krishna's foster-mother that her son was eating earth. Krishna, when questioned, denied it. Yashoda saw Krishna's mouth filled with the whole universe, the earth with all her mountains and rivers and lakes, the moon, the stars and the sun, and she was terrified.

The street we were now passing was bordered by walls on both sides. As little as sixty years ago, this had still been the actual river bed of the Yamuna which had, till then, bordered Vrindaban on three sides. The river has altered its course so much that it now touches the town on one side only. During the monsoons, when the river covers the fields for miles and miles, it returns to its old bed. Then only does one realize the beauty of it all: all the leftover steps and little temples, that had been built at the water's edge, return to life, redis-covering their function. One of these temples sheltered the image of a many-headed snake. Situated under a gigantic Kadamba tree, it was surrounded by a high platform bearing two footprints cut into the stone. 'Krishna's footsteps,' said Dr Govindam, and bent down to kiss them.

'In the river bed of Kalindi – the old name for Jumna – there was a deep hole inhabited by the thousand-headed snake Kalya. The water there was constantly boiling because of the snake's fiery poison, and birds flying over it would fall down dead. When the breeze wafted the poisonous vapours landwards, men, animals and plants died. Shri Krishna, whose mission it was to destroy evil, climbed the Kadamba tree growing above the snake's hole. From there he jumped on to the snake and danced a wild dance on the thousand heads, trampling and crushing them underfoot. All the snake's poison and all its fire were in vain; ultimately, Kalya had to beg for mercy. Krishna relented, as he always did when asked. He did not kill Kalya Nag, but banished him down river, where he could harm Krishna's beloved Braja no more.'

Still the moon shone brightly, but in the east the sky's bluish-white transmuted into reddish-blue. In the trees, birds began to sing, few of them at first, hesitantly, tentatively – but then the voices grew louder, until the air was filled with all the chirping, warble, squeak and rattle.

Dr Govindam hurried us on. We ought to reach the river by sunrise. We passed Madhu Mohan Mandir, situated high up on a steep hill, blackly outlined against a dusky sky. I had often climbed its one hundred steps; the temple is considered the oldest of the large ones here and it is dedicated to Krishna, who even charmed the all-powerful god of love. A friendly old Bengali was in charge there; he had shown me everything there was to see, even the image of Krishna and Radha made of pure silver that is shown only once a year.

We were pilgrims, and pilgrims should not delay unnecessarily. In the tropics, there is no gradual dawn. Night turns into day very rapidly. We were standing at the river's edge, when the sun's red disc slowly slid over the edge of the horizon. Dr Govindam began the samdhya, his morning prayer, said by every brahmin for thousands of years: 'Om. May the splendour of the rising sun illuminate my thoughts. Om!' With his right hand, he scooped some water out of the river, sipped a few drops, did pranayama – closing his left nostril and blowing, with the right one, on the water in his hand, repeated this with the other nostril: thus driving out the 'man of sin' – purifying himself. He sprinkled a few drops on himself, a few drops towards the sun and then, facing the sun, he recited vedic mantras.

It was not because I wished to imitate Dr Govindam, but because I began to understand something, that I folded my hands as well and bowed towards the east, towards the risen, glorious sun. 'Christus Sol' – how little we think uttering these liturgical words, we who live in walled-up religious institutes and hardly remember the existence of a sun, of a moon and of stars, because we are so busy with home-made rules and exercises, with books and with words. Perhaps reality indeed escapes us.

We passed the Keshi Ghat, which is now the most prominent place. It takes its name from another miraculous incident: here, Krishna killed a demon. It has long flights of steps right down to the river, tall buildings and shelters, where pilgrims can rest or dutifully perform their religious rites. At all times of the day, barbers give little boys ritual haircuts prior to the ceremony of the sacred thread. There are always pilgrims who have travelled from afar.

At sunrise, the whole town, spread along the river for more than a mile, awakens to new life. It was six o'clock. The municipal water mains opened their taps for one hour. Twice a day, eagerly awaited by each and everyone, water could be had for one hour. Long rows of men, women and girls had gathered near the taps on the road. It did not take long for the first quarrel to break out. Those standing at the back were under the impression that the ones in front were not in a hurry. In front, three or four were quarrelling about precedence. The discord would last for as long as the water flowed. Everyone was satisfied in the end, except the last few. Water is scarce in Vrindaban.

Not far from the river bank, there was a peepul tree on a slightly raised platform. Long, coloured pieces of cloth fluttered from the branches. They were saris, but it did not look as if they had been hung there merely for the purpose of drying.

Dr Govindam smiled; Mr Sanat grinned impudently. Young girls longing desperately for a husband hang their saris there in the hope that Krishna will send them a good husband. But why here?

'When Krishna had grown to manhood in Vrindaban, one day the young girls of Braj thought of making a vow to the goddess Katyayani: they went on a fast, took a ritual bath in the Jumna, made an image of the goddess out of sand on the river bank, offered incense, flowers and grains of rice and prayed: "Oh goddess, let Krishna be my husband!" Thus they did, day after day, for a long time. Krishna knew about this. So one day, when they had again gone to the river, removed their clothes and were playing in the water, loudly singing the praises of Krishna, he came and took away their clothes and climbed on a nearby tree. He called out to them to come singly and pick up their clothes. The girls were ashamed of their nakedness and did not want to come out of the water. But Krishna did not give in: "If you are my handmaids and wish to do my bidding, then come and take your clothes with a cheerful smile." With their hands they tried to cover their nakedness. But Krishna insisted that they should clasp their hands above their heads, bowing deeply before him. Krishna gave them their clothes. In spite of having been tricked, they did not chide Krishna, but looked on him full of love.'

Mr Sanat laughed; but Dr Govindam explained that we should understand the meaning correctly: anyone who wants to reach God must shed all veils of falsehood and stand naked and free before him.

We turned away from the river and came to an open stretch of land, a stony path between fields, hemmed in by low clay walls and thorny shrubs. It began to be hot. Every step kicked up dust. After a short while we came upon a young man, lying flat on the ground and apparently doing some gymnastic exercises. He got up, reached back with his left hand as far as he could, picked up a stone from a small heap lying there, stretched himself flat on the ground, reached with his right hand forward as far as possible and put the stone there on a similar small heap of stones. After watching this for a few minutes, I asked the meaning of this. Dr Govindam explained to me that the young man was not allowed to speak as long as he was occupied with this especially meritorious form of parikrama. On a particular spot of the parikrama route, 108 pebbles had to be collected and then moved, as shown by the young man, pebble by pebble, the length of the body at a time. After all 108 pebbles have been moved the distance of about two steps, one starts all over again. How long does it take to make the pilgrimage in this manner? Weeks – perhaps months. We passed other devout people who had chosen this penance, among them an old widow. Dr Govindam explained to us that she was probably doing it to gain merit that would profit her husband in the other world.

Truly, I have seldom found such faith! Self-redemption? Penance? Grace? Who can tell! What do we know of the working of divine and human love? Is parikrama done out of love? Is it real love that compels this old woman to take on this strenuous pilgrimage? Weeks later I saw her still at it, a few kilometres ahead of the spot where we had first discovered her. She seemed so weak that after every twenty metres, she remained lying exhausted next to her small pile of stones.

Sevakunj is not situated on the parikrama route, but as we had not yet seen it, Dr Govindam took us on this short excursion. It was a park, according to tradition left as it was in Krishna's time: a wild, fairly high jungle, with thickly interlaced and matted trees and shrubs. The jungle could be crossed only by a roughly paved track that had been kept clear.

Even this path was overgrown with branches and creepers, and one almost had to crawl through it, bent double. Everywhere was full of monkeys. Small ones and big ones, male and female, some of them showing their red naked bottoms in an unmannerly fashion when approached, others spitting and preparing to pounce on us.

In the midst of the wilderness there was a small, strongly built house with a gabled roof. A watchman squatted nearby. He unlocked the bolted doors. In the only room of the little house, there stood a wide bed with pink cushions. The walls were decorated with the usual pictures of Radha and Krishna.

Dr Govindam's eyes lit up. This room in Sevakunj, where Krishna and Radha meet every night for their love-play, is the *sanctum sanctorum* of the holy city of Vrindaban.

Later on, I was to meet a young man who had started off from his village in Bengal, without a penny in his pockets, going to Vrindaban to see the love-play of Radha and Krishna. He had no idea where Vrindaban was, but after weeks of painful touring on foot across the major part of Northern India – it must have been a thousand miles or more – he arrived. He hid in the thick brush of Sevakunj. No visitor is allowed to spend the night here. He endured it for three nights and days, without food. He was an unspoilt young peasant. He did not see Krishna and Radha, and he admitted it. What had he done wrong? Why was Krishna not pleased with him? Krishna himself had said that he would give his bhaktas whatever they asked for. He went to an elderly swami for consolation, and he took him on as a pupil; he would have to prepare himself for the great blessing of immediate divine perception by serving a guru for years, perhaps decades.

In another clearing in Sevakunj we found a round spot, inlaid with mosaic stones. On one side of it was a throne, overshadowed by a strange, bizarre tree. During festivals, this spot was often used for dancing. On the other side, there were small and large samadhis – memorial shrines for great saints who had lived in Vrindaban, poets and singers of the love of Krishna, ascetics who had chastized themselves for Krishna, important preachers of redemption through Krishnabhakti. In front of the biggest shrine stood a flute player, leaning against a coloured pillar. We already knew each other; he had once shown me all his home-made bamboo flutes. In his own way, he was a gifted artist. In him, Krishna's magic flute has returned to Vrindaban.

We continued our pilgrimage. It had grown hot. We again had open land in front of us, sparsely grown with trees and shrubs. I do not know whether it was the heat or the trees that caused Dr Govindam to relate how Krishna had several times saved the cowherds from a forest fire which had surrounded them on all sides and which threatened to suffocate them.

Krishna swallowed the fire, and thus man and beast were saved. The symbol of the forest fire is familiar to the Hindus as the image of the situation of man in this world: samsara is like a forest aflame. The poor human being sees himself inescapably trapped. The miraculous intervention of Krishna saves him; only when God himself consumes the fire is man saved from being engulfed by it.

The largest temple of Vrindaban became visible: Ranganji Mandir, a temple of the Madrasis, built entirely in the South Indian style, with several concentric outer walls, with tall tower-like gate buildings, just like Shrirangam in Tiruchirapalli – only much, much smaller. On both sides of the avenue were lepers – many without fingers, many without toes, others without a nose, without ears – one of them completely faceless: in the middle of his head gaped a large hole, where the stump of a tongue moved; he had no nose, no eyes . . . Almsgiving is also a meritorious deed. Rich people give each beggar a whole loaf of bread or a piece of cloth; less affluent ones give each of them a coin or a few grains of maize. The first wall may be passed by everybody; the large portals were wide open. Inside the first court, there was a pretty mandapam, the usual multi-pillared gallery. Next to it was a large rectangular pond flanked on all sides by flights of steps leading down to it. Two long flat boats were anchored there. On particular feasts, these were decorated and illuminated and the image of God taken around in them.

In front of the second gate in the second wall, guards stood with a large board inscribed in Hindi, allowing only Hindus to enter. They looked at me somewhat doubtfully: now I did not belong to the totally 'white' ones and it was obvious that I was doing parikrama accompanied by two undoubtedly genuine Hindus. Therefore I could pass the small opening in the gate. Inside, there were long colonnades. Within the first part of the courtyard, the garuda-sthambha: a tall gilded metal pillar extending three arms, the landing place for the bird Garuda, the vehicle of Vishnu. On the right, towards the front of the courtyard, was a small shrine with the most sacred object: the image of Vishnu. For his sake, the whole temple had been built. . . . We left the temple by another gate and traversed the outer courtyard with a row of dwellings that house the many brahmin families doing temple service.

We were facing the last lap of our parikrama. Meanwhile, it had grown very hot. When passing the next temple on the way, we asked for some water. It was a Hanuman temple. A large image of the monkey god, the symbol of the imperturbable friend of God, stood in the centre, doused with red paint. Some bhaktas sat in front of it, reciting their morning prayers. An elderly swami gave us water and 'sacrificial food'. We conversed a little and Dr Govindam explained who I was and why I had come. 'Dhanya! Dhanya!' the old swami exclaimed: 'Blessed! Blessed!' A life of brahmacharya, devoted to God, with no other cares and duties except to serve God; that was a really blessed life, so he said. According to him, I must have earned a very good karma in my past life, that it should be given me in this my last life to trek into sacred Vrindaban from faraway Europe. Whoever touches the body of Krishna, i.e. Vrindaban, with his bare feet, is saved. Dhanya! Dhanya! I ought to come and see him now and again.

We crossed a small narrow-gauge railway track and could already see our house, from which we had set out.

The path was bordered by a row of small huts of clay and reeds, where sadhus of all denominations lived. One of them, a ramanandi, whom I knew already, called and waved to me, asking me to enter. He was busy with his religious morning toilet. In the palm of his left hand he mixed white paint, with the right hand he painted parallel white lines on to his forehead and white circles on his chest, arms and thighs – on sixteen particular parts of his body. Then the same in red. White stands for Rama, red for Sita. He explained to me in detail the importance of this ceremony: without these symbols on his body, all the religious exercises, prayers and ceremonies are of no avail. Then he expounded his ideas to me. He wanted to build three temples here, one each for Vishnu, for Shiva and for Brahma. He needed three lakh rupees for the temples, and I should get them for him from rich Europe, or at least ten thousand rupees, that he could build a wall round his plot. He had planted some tulsi trees sacred to Vishnu. The goats had eaten their foliage. Such a crime could easily be avoided with a miserable ten thousand rupees. Wasn't I a sadhu, too? Sadhus should help each other.

When we were leaving, my friend offered me some grey-green globules, a mixture of various narcotics. 'Good for medication,' he said. His neighbour, a member of another sect, was already waiting for us at the door of his hut. 'Don't give him anything, he begs from everybody – he doesn't need anything, don't give anything!' he entreated us.

And then we finally were 'at home' again, back where we started from five hours ago. We had closed the sacred circle; the merit of having visited all the temples of Vrindaban was ours. Before entering the house, Dr Govindam asked us to utter, together with him, a loud 'Jai Radhe' – our homage to Krishna's favourite gopi, our acknowledgement of Krishna's love.

Dr Govindam and Mr Sanat called out loudly 'Jai Radhe'. They looked at me questioningly.

❧ 3 ❧

Talk about God

We had agreed to meet every morning for an hour to discuss a religious subject. We, that is, an elderly Vaishnava swami, a distinguished retired professor of philosophy from Calcutta, a pious, cultured Sikh professor, a one-time government official who was a very eager bhakta, and a young progressive Hindu. And of course, myself.

It took us several weeks to get to know one another's essential background, before we could begin a discussion on basic things without too serious a disagreement. It was as if each of us had to learn several new languages: many of the words we all used and that seemed self-evident to each of us, had a totally different meaning for most participants. Therefore, a large part of our 'dialogue' consisted in simply relating how a particular idea was used in our respective traditions. Each one of us had much to learn, and that was true particularly of me. We had not fixed any particular subjects for our discussion; it appeared that one subject followed another, so that we would grope our way from discovery to discovery. Usually, one of us would begin by relating an event, an experience with someone of another religious community, that had created a problem for him.

This time, the Vaishnava swami began to relate how he had been connected with the Gaudia-Vaishnava mission of Bengal for many years and had travelled in Europe and America as a missionary of Krishna-bhakta. He had been in Berlin for quite some time. It was at the beginning of the Thousand Year Reich, and he had personally met several of the brown gentlemen. He lived with a Jewish family who, one evening, took him to the theatre, to a performance of Goethe's *Faust*. The prologue in heaven was staged thus: under a blue, starry sky a throne, on it a venerable figure in a long white gown, with flowing white beard and slow, dignified movements. The muted voice of God came over a loudspeaker from the wings.

Swamiji thought this a typical Christian conception of God, and a more primitive and less aesthetic one than the god-conception of the Vaishnavas, yet overlapping on essential points: God has a body, God has particular attributes, God speaks to man, God is love. Consequently, it was possible to say that Vaishnavism and Christianity on the one side were opposed to the God-conception of the advaitins on the other side.

At that time, I knew only a little of Vaishnavism, but I thought that here I would have to help out. As far as the theatre went, I pointed out, nowadays many producers had this prologue delivered by a speaker in front of the curtain. It was wrong to regard a theatrical scene as a correct interpretation of Christian theology. 'God is spirit,' I quoted; that was Christian theology. 'God in Christian theology is the Absolute – "*actus purus*", invisible, indivisible, infinite, transcendental.' – 'In that case,' interjected Professor D. (he was a Vedanta Advaita and we called him only 'Shankara'), 'I should say the Christian idea of God is nearer to the Advaita Vedanta than to Vaishnavism: the corporeal God is provisional. The true absolute, which we call Brahman, is pure consciousness, a negation of everything finite, the neti-neti of the Upanishads, the absence of all form.'

Here again it seemed to me that Christianity was misunderstood. 'Christian theology is not content with the neti–neti – God is not provisional, we can make perfectly valid, positive statements on God, having truth value.'

Here, our bhakta cut in: 'Does Christianity have any proper philosophical basis at all? God either has a form, as we Vaishnavas say – or he has none, as the Advaitins say. There is no third possibility. Christianity has no real philosophy; it has taken its teachings from everywhere and justifies them by claiming to possess the only true revelation, to dispense the only salvation. Hence the intolerance, the inability to convince philosophically. Religiously, Christianity is under-developed.'

Swamiji agreed: To be sure, he knew many Christians and also had good friends among them but, religiously, he did not take them seriously. Religion, for them, either consisted of church-going or of social work. Not one of them was capable of conversing on religious themes in any depth. The priests were mostly fanatics.

Now, the modern young man began to speak: 'All representatives of religion are fanatics – and have to be. No religion can be proved by reason. Religion is a derailment of the human mind. If man wants to become free, he has to kill God; God is socially harmful.'

The pious Sikh professor uttered a loud, long sigh: 'Vaih Guru, Vaih Guru, Vaih Guru. . . .' And shielding his mouth with his hand, he whispered in my ear: 'The young man smokes – what can he understand of religion!' Only much later did I understand what he had meant: it is one of the tenets of the Sikhs (and of many Hindu sects) to abstain from smoking. If one of them does it anyway, he excludes himself from the Sikh community, at least theoretically speaking. Hence the aversion to people who smoke.

'Shankara' burst out laughing – he was amused when young people protested against established institutions. He himself mocked the Vaishnavas and their 'beautiful God'. 'All of you Vaishnavas are women,' he had once told the swami openly, when the latter had begun to enthuse about gopi-prema, about the necessity to place himself in the role of a milkmaid, in order to love Krishna completely. In return, he was told that he was an atheist. He had laughed about that, too.

'Vedanta is definitely not a derailment of the mind,' he began to explain. 'Neither is it a "religion" in the sense of, say, Vaishnavism or Christianity. Vedanta is cognition, knowledge of oneself, conquest of illusion, attainment of reality.' The young man was defiant: 'Only what I myself can see and feel is reality. Everything else is illusion, self-deception. The so-called religious people live in a dream land. They deceive themselves. They overlook reality. They are too cowardly to face facts.'

'That's right,' smiled 'Shankara'. In Indian philosophy, this point of view is called Lokayata: 'For as long as you live, be merry. . . . There is no beyond, no God, no return.' But this holds good only as long as you are healthy and well-off. After all, it is only the surface. There is something else, a reality that is different. 'Shankara' is no visionary; Vedanta is a method of recognizing reality, and anyone meeting the conditions can accomplish it: 'Nitya anitya viveka . . .,' he began to quote. 'It requires power of discernment between illusion and reality, self-control and a delight in truth. This is an absolutely rational experience; there are no mythological beings, no fairy heaven as with the Vaishnavas and Christians. The highest is sat-chit-ananda, pure essence, pure consciousness, pure beatitude in conscious existence. The path takes time and calls for effort – but it does not require malas, pujas and murtis.' Again he laughed; he had observed how this worked in Swamiji and in the Bhakta.

Promptly came the reply: 'Advaita is atheism, it is only

veiled Buddhism. This so-called rationality is nothing but unbelief. One cannot know God without faith. He reveals himself only to believers. We need the guidance and writings of those who have been favoured by him. We need the sacred scriptures. Our Bhagavata Purana is the word of God – God is found therein. God can be found in a true guru, not in the abstract speculations of Advaita.'

'Grace of God, revelation, sacred scriptures . . .' – words familiar even to me from the Christian tradition. Yet I did not feel quite at ease with them. I asked for further explanation of the subject.

Swamiji began to relate about Krishna: 'Krishna is God himself – in the Bhagavata God's self-revelation can be seen: he has, at first, shown himself as avatar in many forms, in his full form finally as Vasudeva Krishna, born in Mathura, bred in Gokula and Vrindaban. God has a shining blue body, four arms, around his loins a cloth of yellow silk, a jewel on his breast wherein, at the time of universal sleep, all souls reside. God lives in a palace in heavenly Vaikuntha.' He spoke of his own experience of Krishna. He was about fourteen years old. On his way home from school one day, Krishna met him, coming out of a rice field, just as he had described him. Krishna smiled at him and embraced him. The contact electrified and changed him. 'Since then I had no other thought but to serve only Krishna, and I became a sadhu.' Even now, his eyes shone strangely. No doubt he really had experienced something. All his endeavour belonged to this Krishna. The Sikh professor agreed: 'Religion cannot be proved by logic – religion is inner experience.'

The young man wanted to know how one came by such an experience. He asked derisively what he would have to do to be embraced and changed by Krishna.

'Shankara' laughed again. Swamiji and the Sikh professor

looked shocked. 'Vaih Guru, Vaih Guru, Vaih Guru . . .' – this time it sounded a good deal less gentle.

Swamiji was almost angry. Nevertheless, he managed to set forth the sadhana prescribed by the bhakti acharyas: 'One of the basic exercises is nama-japa, the frequent repetition of one of the revealed names of God: the name of God is God in the form of "shabda" – and the constant repetition brings about a union with God in the shape of the Word.' From there, it was possible to ascend to the real form of God. It was essential to surrender completely to God; that was called sharanagati. In practice, this implies putting oneself under a guru's control and serving him in everything. 'God appears in the guru.' And further, only to take sattvik food, i.e. to follow all the Vaishnava food regulations for at least a year.

The young man did not look particularly cheerful when this last point was mentioned. He thought of his daily meals in the hostel . . . To illustrate the importance of Japa, Swamiji mentioned the example of Ajamila, as it is told in the Bhagavata: a single, unintentional invocation of the name of God in his last hour brought the depraved Ajamila, who despised all morality, straight into Vishnu's heaven, the Vaikuntha. The Bhagavata assures everyone that even an unintentional, unconscious uttering of any name of God, even when stumbling or sneezing, brings mukti without fail.

'Why should a single word be sufficient?' asked 'Shankara'. 'I can say "gold" a thousand times and yet have none.'

Swamiji explained further: God has revealed himself as shabda; only because he has said so, does his name have this effect. He has said nothing of gold. Even in the Bhagavad Gita Krishna promised his worshippers that he would certainly save them should they appeal to him.

'I feel absolutely nothing,' said the young man, 'even if I say "Hare Krishna" a hundred times over.'

'There are two kinds of men,' continued Swamiji irritably, 'some of a divine and others of a demoniac nature. Only those with a divine frame of mind can utter the name of God, only they can believe. The others descend into hell.'

'Shankara' challenged me: 'And what has Christianity to say? Is the shabda-Brahman, the "Word of God", not identical with your Logos in St John's gospel?'

I found it exceedingly difficult to reply. I tried to explain that the meaning of Logos was nevertheless different – less material and less concrete.

'But you believe in a personal God?' 'Shankara' insisted.

'Yes, we do believe in a personal God – but not in a God with a body, a particular skin colour, dress, etc. "Personal", for us, is a spiritual concept, just like the sat-cit-ananda of the Advaitins; that would paraphrase our idea of "Person" rather well.'

'That's what I said,' remarked 'Shankara', 'but – then there can be only one person – there is only one sat-cit-ananda, and we are all identical with it. God and man are one: "Ayam atman brahman".'

'And why shouldn't there be more than one person?' I interjected. 'We are many of us, here – each of us is a person. God is person – different from all other persons.'

'Sat-cit-ananda can be only one: because it is infinite and eternal. Every limitation would be an intrinsic contradiction; finite being is no "being", finite consciousness is no "consciousness", finite salvation is no "salvation". Didn't you yourself say: "God has no divisions"? Brahma is indivisible. As long as divisions can be perceived, as long as plurality can be seen, one remains caught up in illusion, in maya. Reality is one.'

Swamiji began to speak again – he had been silent too long. 'Yes, we believe all is one: God is a large lump of gold, we are splinters; God is fire, we are sparks – one nature, split up into many beings, one in reality.'

'You also say that God consists of three persons?' 'Shankara' asked again. 'I have never been able to grasp this. Isn't this a remainder of polytheism – the old God of Israel, the Christians' new God, Jesus, and Greek philosophy as spirit?'

Where to start with an explanation? No, it wasn't polytheism.

'It is one God – one divine nature – the persons are different in their relationship to each other.' But, here again, I was confronted with the insurmountable obstacle that, for the Advaitin, there simply could not be any kind of plurality, not even of relationships and effects, in sat-cit-ananda; and that the bhakta claimed for every individual the same relationship. For him, the reality of a relationship with God, a personal relationship, is more truly and more deeply evident in Radha and Krishna than in a father-son relationship.

And then, there was this question about the historical Christ: Is Christ God? In that case, does God have a body? God and man in one – is it not an unrecognized insight of Advaita when Christ declares himself to be one with the father – is it not the same as Aham Brahmasmi?

Christ as the son of God is eternal, he has been connected with creation from the very beginning as 'cosmic Christ'. St Paul says: 'He is the image of the invisible God, the first-born of all creation; in him everything in heaven and on earth, all things visible and invisible, have been made . . . everything by him and for him. He is before everything, and everything exists in him.'

'I do not understand this completely,' remarked 'Shankara'. 'You know that our Vaishnava friends here believe the whole world to make up one quarter of God's body – that we consequently tread on a piece of God every time we walk, that we take in a morsel of God each time we eat . . .' It sounded somewhat sarcastic, and I felt sorry that my quotation from the scriptures had been the cause.

Again it was evident to me that I was facing insurmountable hurdles: 'Body' is, for the Advaitin, the absolute opposite of 'spirit'; for as long as there were a 'body consciousness' and a 'body existence', there could be no ultimate cognition, no supreme existence. A God in three persons was provisional – a God with a body was imperfect, mythological.

I tried to speak of faith, of the experience of faith. Of the 'spirit' in the Christian sense, of the reality of creation. 'Shankara' beckoned to me not to say what I was going to say.

'Your Christs and Chaitanyas and Gurus and whatever it is you venerate, they have all been good and dear human beings – but they have all got stuck in the provisional. They have confused the finite with the real, they have not realized the absolute. They are manifestations of Ishvara, if you like, incarnations of the finite creator God. Whatever is tangible and lends itself to description is always finite – always illusion, maya, not being, Brahman. All our real cognition is nothing more than the correction of faulty thinking. We begin to operate with wrong conceptions and ideas. We must pierce maya. Maya is an "illusion of reality" – not its opposite, what you have just correctly described as "image of godhead": an "image", a "symbol", to be understood by overstepping the symbol and recognizing reality.'

Somehow, this thought seemed to me attractive and correct – in spite of relegating Christ to maya. How much of his godhead had been recognized by those who had experienced him in his humanness? Had not Philip said, on the very eve of the crucifixion, that he did not know the Father? Is Godhead as easily recognizable as our schoolbooks profess? Do we know Christ by manipulating a few dogmatic formulas? I felt very small – I knew I had been pushed against a wall too high for me to climb. What was the use of all this beautiful theology I had been studying for years? I would have to learn much, very much, before I could even begin to speak understandably to 'Shankara' and Swamiji about God and Christ.

'Religion is only fit to be fought about; without religion, there would be less war in the world,' the young man professed.

Unfortunately, he was right, even if Swamiji let fly at him on account of his inexperience.

Swamiji, however, began to explain that one would have to rise towards a knowledge of God step by step – that the lower steps would still be littered with misunderstanding, opposition, dispute. This did not speak against religion as such, but against the imperfection of religious men. Atheists agreed even less with each other. The essence of God is love – but the highest step of Prema-bhakti, where all opposites disappear, is granted only to the elect. All religions of the world can be fitted on to one of the steps leading up to Prema-bhakti – only in the love of Krishna and Radha was perfection achieved.

Our bhakta enthused: 'Yes, in Chaitanya alone has the highest religion found its full expression. Christianity with its idea of a child's love for his father is only an aspect; Chaitanya has systematically tried and established the whole step-ladder of "rasas". The lowest love is the love of a servant for his master – a religious man would have to begin with that.' 'Then,' he said, 'came the love of parents for their children – one would have to imagine God to be his child, to be God's father and mother and thus love him. Then, according to the "bhakta", came the love of the child for his parents, the prototype of Christian love. Higher than that was the love between friend and friend – as represented in Krishna and his friends. God places himself on our level. This was – if the

Advaitins were not to be regarded as godless – the Vedanta view: I am as God. But there exists an even higher love, the love of a young woman for her beloved: this prema-bhakti alone can recognize God fully. God is the soul's beloved.'

Is there much sense in setting forth 'Christian love'? Would my intended meaning be grasped if I explained a few more scripture quotations? Had I myself understood yet what it was all about? If I was now to speak of the Holy Spirit as 'love', the Advaitin would bite the bait at once and accuse me of dualistic imperfection, whereas the bhakta would despise me as an undercover Advaitin. Doesn't Christianity in all its assertions presuppose something that remains unsaid? Doesn't it presuppose Christ and his presence?

The hour was up – we had to devote ourselves to other work. We would continue the discussion the next day, probably talking on the same subjects. Had we advanced?

I began to understand much; I had lost much of the theological self-assurance acquired in the seminary. How little we are concerned with God when we speak of God – how much we try to put ourselves into the limelight, even here.

Later I was to have many deep encounters, but we rarely, if at all, spoke of God. Strangely, my friends whom I thus met also told me that, if we sat together silently, they often understood more than if we talked.

The discussion on God did not seem so important, after all.

Theology at 120° F

The weather had been unbearable for weeks now. Although the atmosphere was so dry that book covers turned up at the corners like Japanese gable-ends, we were constantly bathed in perspiration. It was not for nothing that the local people tied a red kerchief round their necks. The walls radiated heat like an oversized central heating system. We spent the nights on open terraces. Concrete floors were hot in the evenings and still warm in the mornings. Unless a soft breeze was blowing, the mosquitoes would torment us. No sooner had the sun lifted itself above the horizon than it became unbearable again. It wasn't so much the heat, as the constant necessity of pitting all one's strength against a hostile atmosphere, just to remain alive. The sun was no more a life-giver, but a murderer. And as yet there was no hope of rain. Even if the monsoons should arrive in time, we had another month to go. And each day would make us more apathetic, till finally nothing mattered any more.

First thing in the morning I celebrate the Mass. I wonder if any person responsible for prescribing the liturgical vestments in use today ever read Mass at 113° F, in a closed room without a fan? Clouds of flies swarm around the chalice and host. They settle on the hands, on the perspiring face. They cannot be driven away, but return for the tenth time to the place from which they have been chased away. The whole body burns and itches. The clothes are damp, even the vestments. They soon dry. If a priest does not wear them all, he commits – according to existing canon law – at least a dozen or so mortal sins all at once. And it seems impossible to survive, physically or spiritually, without the Mass.

Some time before noon, a kind of temple gong resounds. The 'cook' has prepared breakfast. For a year now, there have been no surprises: chapatis, hard, tough, unleavened bread made of wheat flour, smoky tea and some thick, greyish-yellow milk of an uninviting appearance. Sometimes, there is some sugar. Large ants scurry excitedly inside it. In the meantime, the temperature has risen to 117° F. Whatever you touch is sticky with perspiration. Water is scarce. Most wells have only salty, brackish and definitely unpalatable water. Drinking-water comes from a special well. A few months ago, someone fell – or jumped – into it. It took a long time to extricate him. The well is thirty metres deep; the man was dead, of course. It is our only drinking-water well.

Some deadlines are pressing. Some magazine articles have to be finished. The typewriter is hot to the touch. It seems as if even the metal frame is being bent out of shape by the heat. The keys keep getting entangled. The first four litres of water have already been drunk. The stone floor is hot, although untouched by the sun. Heat wafts inside from the open window. The sky is whitish-grey, like glowing iron. Everything is grey in grey – the field, the trees, the clay walls of the houses; the trees have shed their foliage, the fields are interlaced with broad, deep cracks. Desert. For half an hour, one forgets everything and writes. Because a few rupees are needed to make a living. Complaints do not sell easily. So one writes optimistically: about the beauties of India, about the positive chances for the future of the church in India, about the vast perspectives the Vatican Council has opened for the 'dialogue' – things that may find a response in Europe and help to make the holiday a little more interesting. It is not that one finds things amusing; but one laughs any way. If only it wasn't so hot. A well-meaning colleague suggested I ought to take a holiday – in Kashmir, perhaps. With an income of ten pounds a month this is impossible, even in India. After all, we don't work for money. We work for the kingdom of God. Which means a lot of money in some places, none in others.

A short, uncomplicated article on the Christian idea of God had to be done for a Hindu magazine. Nothing modern, something quite ordinary. The subject had been discussed in all the theological textbooks, of course. All that need be done is to argue a few single points a little. However, what was written there and what one had studied with adequate zeal only a few years ago now seemed so inadequate, so irrelevant, so untrue. Theology at 120° F in the shade seems, after all, different from theology at 70° F. Theology accompanied by tough chapatis and smoky tea seems different from theology with roast chicken and a glass of good wine. Now, who is really different, *theós* or the theologian? The theologian at 70° F in a good position presumes God to be happy and contented, well-fed and rested, without needs of any kind. The theologian at 120° F tries to imagine a God who is hungry and thirsty, who suffers and is sad, who sheds perspiration and knows despair. But all this is already too hinduistic.

The theologian at 70° F and with a well-ordered life sees the whole world as a beautiful harmony with a grand purpose, the church as God's kingdom on earth and himself as promoter of the real culture of humanity. The theologian at 120° F sees the cracks in the soil and the world as a desert; he considers whether it wouldn't be wiser to keep the last jug of water till the evening; he wishes the heat was a few degrees less and he has to exert all his Christian faith trying to find a little bit of sense in this life wherein he plays such a very insignificant role, because he depends on so many people.

Towards noon the light discolours strangely. It turns yellow, then dark, then black. And then, things happen very quickly. Within minutes, the temperature drops by almost ten degrees. Doors and windows are shut. There's a whistling and roaring and hissing – all sorts of things fly against the wooden doors and shutters. This is the daily sandstorm. Sand enters everywhere – sand, sand, sand. Sand in the nose, sand in the eyes, sand between the teeth. Sand in the typewriter. Outside, visibility is less than a yard. It doesn't last long. Half an hour, perhaps. Then, everything is as before. And soon enough, we have 120° F in the shade again.

The theologian at 70° F with a well-fed god compiles very nicely what other theologians at 70° F with well-fed gods have written before him. Everything is well documented; the footnotes take up almost half the page. French, English, Latin and Greek authors are quoted. They know exactly that God's grace, like American development aid, is meant for all heathen, for the pro-US ones as well as for the others. The former get a little more. If only everybody follows nicely the road prescribed by their ministers and prelates, there will be enough for everyone. This is very convenient for the 70° F theologians; in that case they do not have to go themselves to where it is 120° F.

Lunch is as it always has been for a year now: chapatis, dal and pumpkin. Because there was a sandstorm, there is sand in the dal and vegetable. It grates a bit between the teeth, but otherwise it tastes as always: of the smoke of a cow-dung fire and of sweat. It is not permissible to eat more than three chapatis, or there will be a quarrel. A professor and a student, both of them Masters of Art and teachers of philosophy, have become inexorable enemies, all because the professor had drunk, in the opinion of the student, an extra cup of tea and without paying for it.

A goatherd with his few goats has sought the paltry shade of a tamarind tree. Goats always manage to find a few twigs on bushes and shrubs. The animals breathe heavily. Somewhat apart, a goat lies in the shade of a small shrub. Crying pitifully, she moves her head, like a pendulum, from right to left, from left to right, from right to left. The crying sounds quite human, like that of a helpless small child. That's what had attracted the theologian's attention. The animal probably suffered from heat-stroke. And then there was a rustle in the air. The first vultures arrived in low flight, brushed past the goat, hopped up and down a few times, used their wings as brakes and sat down nearby. The goatherd dozed, leaning against the tamarind tree. It did not worry the other goats. More and more vultures arrived. They seemed to drop out of the hot, leaden sky – the embodiment of the sun's cruelty. And still the goat was wailing; more and more her cries resembled those of an infant. The vultures sat around in a circle, sometimes stretching their necks and looking at the dying animal.

The fever ate into the theologian's consciousness. He did not know his whereabouts any more. Around him a few figures – sometimes they seemed to have human faces, but then he saw the long naked necks and the vulture beaks. A racking pain in the head – one of the vultures must have hacked into it. And once again. The vulture had a spiteful face. 'What good has all this done you? If only you had stayed at home!' Another one pecked. Where had he seen that face before? 'Had you been reasonable,' that one said, 'you could be one of us and well off.' Again another one pecked – a vivid pain shot through the eyes. And then it felt as if a piece was torn out of the intestine. The face seemed familiar. 'Now we've got you,' said the vulture, laughing. A new pain distracted the theologian from his brooding. Another vulture had pecked at him. They quarrelled with one another, and then hacked and pecked alternately. Sometimes, everything grew hazy in front of his eyes, but then again he could clearly distinguish the faces. They were all there, now. The pain in the ears was new. Suddenly he became aware of it as sounds. When he is well, he calls it music. The clear, high tones were like stings in the head now; the darker notes were more bearable. Ah! yes, they were Christmas carols from a tape recorder. He couldn't say that he was glad or that he found it particularly elevating that this was supposed to be Christmas. But he managed somehow to thank those who had installed the tape recorder. They were happy in the knowledge of having done a good deed.

The vultures worked systematically. They began to work on the goat from the back up. The naked long red necks disappeared in the goat's belly; it was horrid and abominable. When one of the birds had torn off a large piece, the others would pounce on it, setting off a wild squabble. They beat each other with wings and beaks. Evidently, they did not agree either.

Again, a furious pain shot through the brain. Then the theologian remembered where he had seen this before. The howling worsened, the nose grew longer and longer, the neck ever thinner and the red of the neck stronger; the eyes burned unbearably. He became afraid. And then, another blow.

The goat was now almost hollowed out. The skin hung loosely on the skeleton. Some of the vultures already sat in the shade, digesting. They had probably had enough. They were fanning gently with their wings. It seemed too hot even for them. It was still 120° F in the shade. Some of the vultures were still busy. Suddenly, they screamed. The street curs had discovered that there was some entertainment to be had. They almost got one of the vultures. A dog had him by the wingtip and dragged him around. With his free wing, the vulture belaboured the attacker. The dogs began to tear up the goat's skin. Some of the vultures swooped down on them, trying to chase them away.

Again this fierce pain. The theologian had already seen this fleshy red face somewhere. Where? The bloodshot eyes, the features distorted with ire – he was overcome by nausea. He wanted to strike at random. But he could not, he was not permitted to do so. The cur bit again.

The dogs had torn the skin and nibbled at it. A great big yellow dog burst in. The small dogs howled and ran off. The vultures had lost all interest in the goat. Most of them now sat near the other goats who were dozing away. Both sides had eaten their fill; they no longer had to be afraid of each other. The goats were glad that the vultures were quiet. A few vultures flew up briefly and then dropped again, using their wings as brakes.

The big yellow dog must have had sharp teeth. He was not cynical, like the vultures; his face was full of self-confidence. He was the lord of dogs. He was stronger than the others, and they ran away from him. Whatever he could crush with his teeth, belonged to him. By right. Because the stronger one has right on his side. Who makes the law? The strongest one. It was impossible to prove the contrary to him. With all the clever things he had learnt, with all the noble convictions with which one had grown up, with all the faith in the reality of the spirit he had to permit the big, strong, yellow dog to bite through his cervical vertebra. And the pain was so terribly near, so terribly real. Much more real than the Christmas carols still flowing from the tape.

In the meantime, night had fallen and the sky was so full of floating dust that the stars were almost imperceptible. The vultures had retired to their tree. Somewhere the dogs lay, resting from their hard day's work. But where the goat had died, there was no rest yet. There was a crackling as of splintering wood. The jackals had stronger jaws than the dogs. The dogs were afraid of them. The jackals had even more right than the dogs, because they could bite even better. They could even manage the bones the dogs had been compelled to leave. They howled. Perhaps they needed to encourage themselves, perhaps they were afraid of someone even stronger than they. It sounded so horrible and so near. They stood directly in front of the house. And howled.

The howling grew to nerve-racking proportions. He knew what would follow. Beginning with the flak. Then the bombs fall. He is afraid – not with a human fear. An animal fear for life, so valueless, so superfluous, so cheap. The age of mass man calls for means of mass destruction. Bigger and bigger bombs. Atom bombs – world bombs. There was howling in the air; the walls trembled. Dust drizzled down. Another sandstorm. This time by night. The ghostly moon seemed almost blue-grey. He pulled the sheet over his head and waited for it to be over.

The fever yielded. Now, he would not mix up things again. The thing with the bombs and the flak – that had been more than twenty years ago; the typhoid and the hospital had also happened a few months back. The goats – well, that was commonplace. An everyday occurrence. Goats are goats. Nothing is left of yesterday's goat. The theologian was supposed to continue writing his theological article.

The next day would be just like this one. Equally hot. As many flies. As much quarrelling about some smoky chapatis and some tea. Goats would continue to die of sunstroke, some men would again be hit by heat-stroke. There would be a sandstorm. Vultures and dogs and jackals would manage dead goats. Dead men could be cremated. Nothing would remain of the goats and their lament, nothing of the men and their suffering. Death was only the other side of life. One did not know which side was the better one – both were dark.

God was the creator and preserver and destroyer. The reason for placing creatures in a desert, in a cruel world, in death – that was his caprice, his play, his lila. First he had created the sun who would one day kill the goat he had also created. He had created the vultures who would consume the goat. The dogs and jackals who would tear the skin to pieces and crack the bones with their teeth, they were also his creatures. *One* atman in all of them – in God and in the vulture, in the goat and in the dog. And also in the one who watched all this, trying to understand. God was the kind mother – and the bloodthirsty goddess of destruction. When misfortune goes on increasing, when catastrophe breaks all bounds, it is imperative to sacrifice to the goddess: her long tongue hangs bloodthirstily from her mouth, she holds a bloodstained sword, cut-off heads and arms are hanging decoratively over her naked breasts. Life issued from God's countenance – death from his back. God is the sacrificer and the sacrifice. Goat and vulture are his manifestations – adoration is due to both.

On the opposite side of the road, there was a longish, brownish something. It was five o'clock in the morning – still twilight. It could have been a buffalo calf, dead of heatstroke. Young buffaloes are very sensitive; they can bear neither heat nor cold, and if one is unkind to them, they fall ill. Every summer, many young buffaloes die of heat-stroke. The chamars would skin them and eat their flesh, because they were an unclean caste. They would not leave the young buffaloes to the vultures and dogs. But the long brown something was not quite dead yet. It was moving very slowly. It was a naked young man, lying in the gutter with his face down. With the hollow of his right hand, he began to pour the waste water over himself: a ritualistic action he felt duty bound to perform each morning. The bhangis then arrived on the scene, the removers of filth, another unclean caste. With long brooms some of them swept the filth accumulated during the night into the gutters. Others poured water from goatskins they carried, washing the excrement down to the river. Thick and black the water came down the gutter. The young man filled his hand with it and poured it over his head. Slowly, the thick pulp divided and crumbled over his face. And then, he took another handful and brought it to his mouth, struggling to make it go down. But the stomach revolted – he had to vomit. A second handful. He cringed with nausea. However, the stomach did not resist any more. The man gulped down one handful after the other of the thick, black, stinking filth.

The children came to life. They fetched long sticks to tease him with. At first, he did not move, Then he charged the children, who ran towards the houses, screaming; the naked young man ran after them, but the door was held fast from the inside. He leaned and pushed against it. Somebody threw a bucketful of filth on him from above. From a window, somebody beat him with a stick till he left the door.

Was he a saint? One of the unmattas? One who wishes to prove by this behaviour that literally everything is Brahman – that God is in the filth as well as in the bread, in madness as well as in reason? There are still many aghoris, adorers of Shiva, who live near burning ghats by preference and even eat human corpses. Would he find Shiva by this means, the God who is life in front and death behind, who capriciously creates and destroys, who, dancing, procreates and kills.

They have an easy time, the 70° F theologians. They settle

down in some library and find enough books there by means of which it can be proved that the non-Christian religions are the normal way to salvation for the non-Christian, that each one finds God even without mission – that one should not disturb the conscience of a non-Christian. In Europe's libraries no goats die of heat-stroke, there are no vultures and no dogs eating the goats. Nor would an aghori be admitted there. Many a thing looks different when seen from a European library – more beautiful, more pleasant, and more abstract. It is a well-known fact that paper is patient – more patient than people, at any rate. The newest theology has discovered that it is quite possible to theologize without God. Perhaps God isn't present any more in the libraries and in the theological colleges, but in the desert – alone. These thoughts must seem absurd to a 70° F theologian. He has his position, his science, his social duties. His students will repeat, during their examinations, exactly what he has taught them. Is God bound to libraries and theological faculties? Will the God of the air-conditioned libraries redeem him who dies of heat-stroke in the desert? Will he be able to drive away jackals, dogs and vultures? But it is a dogma, isn't it, that God offers his grace to everyone? How surprising, then, that Christ should have tired himself out, exposed himself to heat and cold and advocated a very unconventional theology, that he did not care one little bit what politicians and prelates of his time considered reasonable and right! How strange that he did not rely on the fact that God would redeem the world in any case, that he himself should go through the fire of death and find his God in the ultimate solitude of agony! How strange that he should have asked his disciples to do as he had done, that he should have prophesied to them that they would act and suffer like him! How peculiar, that he should have enjoined upon them to preach the kingdom of God and not to presume it! How strange that he did not call scribes and pharisees blessed, but the hungry and thirsty ones! How strange all this . . . !

Many hundreds of millions of people have to live where the temperature is 120° F in the shade, where there are dogs and jackals. A contemporary Indian writer once reflected upon the question whether human beings were so corrupt because the gods of the Indian heaven were so corrupt, or whether the corruption of the gods had its origin in men's corruption. No, says the 70° F theologian: neither men nor gods are corrupt. Things have to be looked at from the right angle. Seen in proper perspective, there is little difference between 120° F and 70° F. If the situation is handled properly, vultures and dogs and jackals can be kept in a zoo; it is even possible to charge an entrance fee to visitors. No, nothing is quite as bad as it looks.

The short, uncomplicated article for the Hindu magazine was finally completed. It turned out somewhat shorter than originally intended, and it contained little of what is found in schoolbooks. The 70° F theologians would say that what was described there was Hinduism. But the people who were Hindus even at 120° F knew better. It was a stirring afternoon, when he read out the article in a seminar. 'Have you noticed how the faces changed during your lecture?' a visiting friend remarked. He had seen it. It was the parting of the spirits. The God manifested in Jesus Christ is no God of libraries and theologians. As such he could fit very well into a Hindu library. But the God who appeared in Jesus Christ is where people suffer and struggle and thirst and hunger. He is a provoking God. He is a God who can cope with vultures and dogs and jackals. He is a God indifferent to nothing; on the contrary, he is light and life and the inexorable enemy of darkness and death. The God manifest in Jesus Christ is not one who watches from afar and develops a new theory about God, but he is a living God, a God who proves to the world that there is sin and justice. He is a God become man not in the circles of pharisees and politicians, but in those circles where hunger and thirst, toil and work, grief and death are well-known. He did not appeal to his divinity but gave his humanity for his brethren. Perhaps the people living in a temperature of 120° F in the shade, where there are vultures and jackals, are also in need of one who, of his free volition, will take upon him what, to them, is cruel destiny; perhaps they are in need of one who will deliver them from the caprice of gods and men; perhaps they are in need of one who knows that life is better than death, that God and Satan are not one and the same. Perhaps they are in need of a God who follows them right into death, when all the beautiful speculations burst like a soap bubble and nothing remains but a dirty little drop of water. He would not give them air-conditioners so that they, too, could live at 70° F, nor guns with which to shoot vultures and jackals. But he would bring them the consolation Christ had brought, a consolation that has little to do with what the world considers consoling. And they would understand. Better than the 70° F theologians. He would not, like the 70° F theologians, bring the superficial peace of theological coexistence. He would bring the sword, the decision, and yet the peace unknown by the world. He does not condemn anyone! Men condemn themselves. He does not deprive anyone of peace. Men deprive themselves of it. He does not reject anyone. Men reject him, because he unmasks their lies and hypocrisy, because he cannot be bribed. They would be willing to place him next to the gods, to offer him incense, even a little money, to cleanse themselves of sin. They would like to have him as a statue – but not as a man, not so immediate and provoking. They would like to have him as a book, for completeness' sake. If the book is interpreted correctly, one only finds what one already knows anyhow.

In the small cubicle euphemistically called 'bath' lay a snake. It had begun to feel too hot in its hole on the parched field. It was a bit damp in the bathroom. We arrived at a friendly understanding. Twice a day, the human beings should be allowed to use the bath. For the rest of the time, the snake was permitted to live there, till the arrival of the rains. Then, a rat arrived. Snakes and rats don't agree either. But both stand in the temple.

Yoganandaji, my brother

The first time I met Swami Yogananda Tirtha, one cool October morning, he was doing his outdoor exercises. He came into our garden, because no one disturbed him there, and he did his physical exercises for half an hour to keep himself supple and healthy. We were of about the same age and were interested in each other. I learnt that he was one of the Dasha-nami Samnyasis, disciples of Shankaracharya. He was never seen standing about the market-place, like so many other sadhus; he was almost always occupied with his studies and his daily, spiritual work. A few weeks after that first accidental meeting we met again at the Manav Seva Sangh; the founder, Swami Shraddhananda, had come to Vrindaban for a few days, and some of my friends who belonged to the Manav Seva Sangh had taken me along to introduce me to the Swami. He was a blind, simple old man and spoke in few and simple words of essential things. Whether it was in my honour that he spoke of Francis of Assisi and Jesus of Nazareth, or whether he did so even otherwise, I do not know. In any case, I again met Swami Yogananda there, and at once we got into an animated discussion on what we had just heard. Swami Yogananda wanted to know whether we could not meet for Bible satsang – i.e. meet daily over a longer period in order to read the Holy Scriptures together and meditate on them. 'Satsang' is the Hindu expression for it, and the method appeared good to me: someone who knows the text well and tries to live accordingly, explains it to others, to whom it is unknown.

I accepted willingly. So Swami Yogananda came to me, every day before sunrise. He wanted 'the heart of Jesus', he said. I was not to give him an authoritarian or theological exegesis, but a mystical one. He already knew the texts fairly well but admitted that he did not feel satisfied with what he had read till now. What attracted him especially was the gentleness of Jesus, his patience and his sacrifice. He considered the Sermon on the Mount to be the 'highest philosophy'. Meditation on Christ's suffering gave him more strength than anything else.

I began by reading the Gospel according to St John with him. Before we began talking, we quietly prayed for enlightenment. We began with the prologue – and he explained to me later that he had meditated for three full days on the mystery of the emergence of the Word from the Father and of the Spirit from the Son and Father, and had experienced deepest bliss while doing so. 'It was the most blissful revelation of my life,' he said. He brought me a book by Billy Graham, the famous evangelist, which he had read. Till then I had scarcely concerned myself with Billy Graham, but found him now to be a typical Unitarian, i.e. he did not recognize a trinitarian God. Yogananda wished to know whether this, too, was Christian. What confusion we cause! I also began to understand during this Bible satsang the impossibility of our Bible translations. Not even one essential term was translated in such a way that a Hindu from his background could understand unambiguously what it was all about. Not only did Yogananda have difficulties owing to his Advaita background; others, like him, complained repeatedly that the Hindi of our Bible translations was 'no Hindi', but a 'foreign language'. The translators knew the grammar and the dictionary, but not Hinduism.

Some of the difficulties he had are likely to be encountered by all Advaitins: he, too, understood 'I and the Father are one' as being an 'Advaita experience' of Jesus. He, too, interpreted the last words on the cross: 'Father, forgive them for they do not know what they do' as Advaita: as the persecutors only saw maya, the body of Christ, they were ignorant of the real essence of Christ. Christ had not really died . . . But again and again his questions showed how deeply he considered these things, and I began to understand the problems that await us if we try to convey the message to the true Hindus. Once, a somewhat distrustful fellow-lodger joined us; he wanted to know what we were doing. It was, after all, immaterial to what religion one belonged. Anyone could find God. Yoganandaji replied that he would not hesitate to confess himself a follower of Christ openly if he was convinced of the truth of Christianity.

The stories of the calling of the apostles gave us the idea of speaking about our own. I asked him to tell me how and why he had become a Samnyasi.

He had been brought up in one of the larger towns in Maharashtra, and even as a boy he felt somehow attracted to the Sanyasis. He went to school, left college as a Bachelor of Arts and took up a job in Bombay. In his spare time he took lessons in painting. Later he showed me some of his work – pictures of Hindu saints, well-done and expressive. Still he thought about becoming a Samnyasi.

His parents, like all parents the world over, had marriage plans for him. But he chose Samnyasa. His departure from home was not as dramatic as in many other cases. He was twenty-eight years old. His parents accepted the fact that their son wished to become a Samnyasi. 'At that time, I found myself in a state of the highest bliss,' he said reflectively, 'I was indescribably glad, and exulted. I let everything just happen. My clothes, my pilgrim's staff, my drinking vessel – everything I gave away. I needed nothing. When someone had given me food and a hungry dog or a crow begged from me, I gave it to them and was happy if they accepted it. If I was presented with a piece of cloth, I passed it on to the next beggar. I was never conscious of needing anything. I felt myself at one with everything, as nature, without any plans, without any interests. I felt at one with the river along which I wandered – it flows on, carries boats and lets the children swim, allows water to be taken and poured into it; it flows on and on, considering it the most natural and self-evident thing in the world simply to love everyone and everything, and it was clear to me that love is the real and deepest essence of things. For eighteen months I trekked like this through India, here and there; I went with anyone who invited me. I thought to myself: is it not the supreme freedom to have no attachments, not even to this body that is transitory and corruptible? I decided to give up eating and drinking. I wandered along the Ganges, upward, into the Himalayas. One day, during my daily bath in the Ganges, I was again strongly overcome by this consciousness of being one with all, as if there was no difference between me and the river, as if my body would flow away into the infinite. But I resisted the temptation to let myself be carried away, and I walked on, up the mountains, into the beautiful landscape beyond Rishikesh. I wanted to "cross" into the endless; into the ultimate freedom, into freedom from the fetters of the body. For days I wandered on, without food and without drink. I met panthers and bears – none hurt me, I had no fear. I did not meet any man in all those days. I re-member that every now and then my strength left me, that I fainted away and then walked on again, as if in a dream. I only remember that, one day, I suddenly awoke to find a sadhu of about sixty sitting near me. In his hand he held a goblet full of milk which he was trying to make me drink. I just let things happen. Without asking any questions he told me, without censure but firmly and definitely, that, in this way, I could not attain what I was striving for. I could not force union with the absolute; I would have to mature and change in a life-long endeavour. The awareness of reality would have to come about naturally, as if on its own; all we could do was to prepare the way for it. I asked him to accept me as his pupil, his chela. I was his only one. After about three weeks of life together, when I had recovered my strength, my Guru explained to me that he did not wish to tie me to him and that I was free to go and come as I pleased. The familiarity of daily life would show the foibles of each person and be a hindrance to my development. I left him with the impression of leaving a dream world, as if awakening from some kind of ecstasy. I knew that the goal I had seen in my "delirium" was right; man should spend himself like a river, he should make it his nature to love and give; but the way I went about it was wrong. It is easy to get rid of the body physically; it is much more difficult to transform the body into an instrument of divinity.'

Swami Yogananda had allowed me to look deeply into his soul. Had I, at the same time, also had a glimpse of the soul of India?

He asked me about my vocation. I told him of my family, of my home, of the school, of the war and the post-war period, of encounters with people, of the slow maturing of the vo-cation, of the seminary and of the studies, of beautiful and of bitter days. I could tell him nothing sensational; I did not wish to impress him. And yet he was deeply moved. How much alike the human heart was, everywhere! By telling one another of our vocation, we had really become brothers. Day after day we held our Bible satsang in this manner. Those hours of meditation and consideration were beautiful and profound beyond all description. No discussions, no comparisons – only a striving for insight. Never before had I understood so well what it meant that He was in the midst of those who, by twos or threes, gather in His name.

Once my brother Yogananda came in the evening. I guessed something had happened. He seemed troubled. His Guru, the old man who had found him in the Himalayas, had sent for him. The Guru was old and feeble and he had no other disciple. Yogananda would have to go to Nasik and he obeyed his Guru – not without regret, because our Bible satsang, so profitable to both of us, had come to an end. But next morning he came once more. He had given away all his books and asked me for a gospel harmony. On the cover page of this he had asked me to stick a picture of the Crucifixion, which he had grown to like. This book and the *Imitation of Christ* he wanted to take with him on his long journey – nothing else.

'Our life, too, must be crucified, every moment of it,' he said softly. He asked for a few words: what Jesus might have said to a Sanyasi. We promised not to write to one another but to wait and see whether God would let us meet again. The monk should have no human attachments. And then he went on his way, a thousand miles on foot.

During the following weeks and months I often caught myself involuntarily looking for Swami Yogananda amidst the numerous Sanyasis. Sometimes I almost believed I had discovered him, and was joyous that he should have returned. But I was mistaken. When, after two years, I left Vrindaban for Bombay, I had given up hope of ever seeing him again. Who can find an acquaintance among five hundred million people in India? But I could not forget him.

I went to Benares in connection with a meeting. It was the time of the kumbhamela in nearby Allahabad, and Benares was incredibly overcrowded. Near the station, I got into a bus for Gudolia; the wrong bus, as I was later to discover. I had just squeezed myself into a seat, when a sadhu came up to me with uplifted hands: 'Klaus, my brother . . . !' he exclaimed loudly. I was speechless. It was Yogananda. We had not seen each other for more than three years; he was just travelling to Gaya. He had been to the kumbhamela and he was making a little excursion to Benares. Utterly without a plan . . . It did not matter to me at all that I had taken the wrong bus; for me there could not have been a righter one. Then Yogananda told me briefly what had happened during those three years, how often he had thought of me and how he had tried unsuccessfully to trace me. He had been living in a small village in Maharashtra for about a year now, seventy miles from Bombay. He gave me his address.

On my return to Bombay I found a letter from Yoganandaji. I was to come to his village as soon as possible and spend a week with him. If that was impossible, then *he* would come. I asked him to come to Bombay. For half a day, we were busy exchanging experiences. Yoganandaji had moved around very much. He had, among other things, undergone a lengthy maun-sadhana, a period of silence. For this purpose, he had gone to Rajasthan, into a forest. The people of a nearby village warned him: not long ago, another sanyasi, who had attempted a maun-sadhana there, had been devoured by a lion. The lion was still in the forest, and no villager ventured into it after nightfall. Yoganandaji was not at all impressed. He wanted to start his maun-sadhana in the very hut where the other sadhu had been eaten up. The people promised to leave a meal for him every day, at the edge of the forest. He spent quiet days in the forest. At night he heard the lion's roar. But that did not disturb him at all. Then, one night, the lion grew bolder. Yoganandaji concentrated on his mantra: 'Shivo'ham – I am Shiva, the eternal, immortal . . . my real being is one with Shiva, the body is not my Self.' Fearlessness is the first sign of union with Shiva. The lion came nearer, circled round the hut, sniffed and growled. 'Shivo'ham,' Yoganandaji repeated again and again, 'Shivo'ham, Shivo'ham, Shivo'ham . . .' The lion entered the open door of the small hut. His powerful head stood clearly silhouetted against the night sky. He growled dangerously. 'Shivo'ham, Shivo'ham, Shivo'ham.' Then he lowered his head and nuzzled Yogananda's foot. At that moment, Yogananda felt as if he had had an electric shock; the lion howled and left the hut, Yogananda broke into a cold sweat and trembled all over his body with fear. He was incapable of repeating 'Shivo'ham'. Now he laughs when speaking of it.

Then he had again gone on a pilgrimage, and during a two weeks' meeting of the Warkaris in Dehu a few men had invited him to come to their village and build his hut there. They gave him land; a friend built him a small Shiva temple which also served him as bedroom and study. Two square yards, that was enough.

I was moved when he told me that he had thought of me whenever he felt very depressed, and that the thought of me had given him courage. When leaving he mentioned that he had thought he could quench his mental thirst by meeting me in Bombay, but that thirst had only increased. So I would just have to spend a few days with him. I promised him this. As soon as I could free myself, I went to him. He met me at the station with a few of his friends from the village, simple, young and upright farmers who, every evening, sang spiritual songs with him and whom he initiated into spiritual life.

He had arranged a small, empty bungalow for us, for three days. A friend from Poona, whom he had told about my forthcoming visit, had sent huge baskets of food. He knew of my love for music, so he had brought three bhaktas from the village who, each morning and evening, played and sang and recited bhajans for several hours. Even now their melodies haunt me.

We spent the whole day near the lake and spoke of the inner life. Still he desired to be completely overcome by God, to see God in ecstasy. He considered himself unworthy and unclean. He asked me again to show him the Christian sadhana, the way to God Christ had taught. He had been occupied for some time with studying and commenting on the Gita. Every day he would do one verse. In the morning he would meditate, in the afternoon read others' commentaries, and in the evening he would write down his own thoughts. He showed me some books filled in his delicate handwriting. It was the sum total of his experience with God. He showed me his Shiva, a small marble statue. He had made arrangements to illuminate the statue from several sides: each time Shiva looked different – threatening, smiling or absorbed. Yoganandaji could meditate for hours in front of Shiva.

One afternoon we climbed over the mountain at the foot of which we then camped, with a view to seeing the famous Buddhist caves in Karla. We walked for an hour and a half. The way led through sparse forest. Nomadic tribes still live there and gather some wood and grass on the slopes, to sell it afterwards. They have no houses and no cattle. But they are strong and friendly. Karla itself is an experience, especially the large Chaitya hall.

We rested in one of the largest assembly halls. Yoganandaji recited in his agreeable voice the three jewels of Buddhism: 'Buddham saranam gacchami, dhammam saranam, gacchami, sangham saranam gacchami.' A muffled echo answered from the empty cells.

The men from the village, invited by Yoganandaji, insisted upon arranging a celebration in honour of my visit. They fetched us in their ox-carts. We had to visit each house in the village. Not one of them was rich, but all were clean and friendly. The children were at first somewhat shy, but they were soon at ease. The food, as always, was excellent and served with great love.

It was not easy for me to say good-bye. They took me to the station in an ox-cart. As many as could possibly squeeze into the cart came along. The trip did not last long; the oxen were good runners. Before reaching the station, we saw another ox-cart. The proprietor had just got off and busied himself at the nearby river. Our driver, who knew the oxen, called to them, 'Ho! Ho!', and the animals started moving with the empty cart, towards the village. Soon, the proprietor came and wanted to see what the matter was. He ran after us, shouting.

As the train was leaving, all of them stretched their hands towards me, all at once: I was to return soon, Swami Yoganandaji had been so glad, and they with him.

Since then he has begun another year's maun-sadhana. When this is over, I shall visit him again.

Sometimes I take his last letter into my hands: 'He Nilakantha,' he has written at the top: 'O Shiva, the blue-throated!' – 'My dear brother,' the letter started, 'My brothers from the village and myself, we would all like to see you again. You must come soon. We shall fetch you from the station with an ox-cart. I have much to discuss with you. I am troubled. With love and greetings, your brother Yoganand.'

The Pilgrim's Progress

The Delhi-Calcutta-Janata train, with only third-class compartments, was, as always, overcrowded. The passages and floor spaces in between the compartments had long been occupied. The doors were blocked with mounds of tin trunks and crates – anyone who wished to enter or leave had to make use of the not-too-large windows. Those who had had the good fortune of being first had made themselves comfortable on the seats. They had spread their bed-rolls and dozed away. Nobody and nothing could make them pull up their legs even by a hand's breadth. Even mothers with little children on their hips, standing in front of them for hours and almost unable to stand straight for sheer fatigue, did not disturb them in the least. On the contrary, they became aggressive if someone tried to commandeer a corner of the bench.

A small boy squeezed himself through the squatting, reclining, standing human cluster. 'Polish! Polish!' he called in his bright voice. He wanted to polish shoes. Business suffers from the fact that, as yet, most people do not wear shoes. Nevertheless, there is many a shoe-owner in the faster trains and, therefore, also many a shoeshine boy, each with small cloth bags containing two brushes, two tins of polish and a few rags – a very mobile and attentive customer service which not one wearer of shoes escapes. The treatment costs 15 paise. The small boys are artists; with zeal and devotion they fetch the last lustre out of old, worn-out shoes. Most of them have lost their parents – and so they live and work in the trains and on station platforms.

A fat fellow in our compartment wore shoes – beautiful light-coloured shoes. Our small shoeshine boy saw them at once. He began to polish them, with ardour. They shone as though new, and the boy pointed this out to their possessor with a kind of artist's pride. He wanted 15 paise – perhaps he counted on a little more; the fat one seemed to have it. But he gave him only 12 paise, saying he had always paid two annas only. More he would not give. The boy stretched out his hand and said, 'Another three paise.' The fat one pretended not to have heard. When the small polish-wallah insisted, he turned wild. He never gave more than two annas, on principle. The child's eyes began to flare – with an expression of utter disdain he flung the two annas on the floor, spat on them and disappeared. The fat man calmed down gradually – and retrieved the two annas.

People grumbled, people criticized, but nothing more. A young man next to me said with contempt: 'You see, father, these are our capitalists.' Because, for a foreigner, it is better to be prudent, I did not want to take him up on the capitalists but asked him whether he was a Christian, since Hindus don't usually address a priest as 'father'. No, he was no Christian. Nor was he a Hindu. He had been to a Jesuit school in Calcutta, and he spoke of the Jesuits with respect. He looked like a high school teacher and was a member of the CPI. The link of St Xavier's College with the Communist Party was still new to me. He saw my surprise. He had nothing against priests or Christians in general. He recognized their idealism, their work and their devotion. 'But we need more – stronger stuff. Christianity is reactionary, always defends the status quo, is too involved with capitalism. Christianity cannot help us any more. The God of the Christians doesn't impress our capitalists, humanism and justice even less. Only money and massive power. Have a good look at Calcutta!'

Worn and overtired after thirty hours' journey I got off the train and was at once received by my swami, accompanied by a nice, simple-looking gentleman. There were the usual garlands for a welcome; then we got into the not-so-new car of the gentleman who wished to be our host in Calcutta. Swami had invited me to accompany him on his birthday tour, prepared by his disciples and friends in his native Bengal. This included a few days in Calcutta.

Our host was a well-to-do businessman: his family were trustees of a temple to which belonged some land and several shops in a city street. He had his own business and managed the temple property. Part of it had to be used, according to the contract, for a major folk festival each year. We were well entertained in a friendly manner. For the people of Calcutta, nothing in the world excels Calcutta. For a foreigner, the city is shocking.

With a strange feeling in the pit of the stomach one refuses the offers of rickshaw coolies. In Calcutta, there are still thousands of those two-wheeled buggy-like rickshaws that are pulled by a man who walks between the harness poles. We refuse, because we cannot bear it that a poor devil, dripping with perspiration, should pull us along a road we can very well walk. And the poor devil loses 25 paise's worth of his earnings.

Human power is cheap in Calcutta – cheaper than diesel oil. There are many heavy, two-wheeled carts with long bamboo ladders piled high with tons of grain, oil canisters, crates of vegetables and bales of cloth – pulled and pushed by six or eight men dripping with perspiration. There is a dearth of accommodation in this largest town of continental Asia. After the partition of India, millions of refugees poured into the city. Millions of people from the neighbouring province look for a means of livelihood. Many of them manage to construct for themselves a hut of crates, cardboard and bamboo matting in one of the large slum areas. Many thousands camp night after night on the footpaths. All their belongings are wrapped in an old blanket.

Poverty and misery are glaring – equally glaring is wealth. Enormous business is transacted in this important harbour town with its ten million people. Thousands become millionaires. Some have good taste and furnish their flats with an artistic flair. Others are primitive. They dismiss you with an oily, cunning smile.

The holy cows trot sullenly through the overcrowded streets, rummaging in the heaps of rubbish in search of something eatable. They even eat paper. People who cannot walk and have no home lie in the streets. Some passers-by throw coins in their tin mugs. Children come and beg. We distribute small coins. This attracts more children and finally we are surrounded by a mob of children between the ages of four and ten, and they give us no peace.

The communist in the train had said that, in India, one had to have a constant bad conscience if one lived in a decent flat, had a good suit of clothes in one's cupboard and palatable food. Communism would abolish bad conscience.

A little girl sat at the street curb, happily engaged in taking peanuts from a small paper bag and nibbling them. A small possession; a small feast. From the rear, an elderly monkey came with blinking eyes and a bare red bottom. The situation seemed to amuse him. Before anyone realized what was happening, he took one leap and grabbed the paper bag full of peanuts from the little girl. It took a moment before the child realized the full impact of the incident. The monkey sat on a wall and gobbled up the monkey nuts in a businesslike manner, winking with his eyes. The girl broke into a storm of tears. Little girls' tears do not move a monkey. He had his peanuts – that was enough. Animals, too, are cruel. Have they learnt cruelty from man?

We left Calcutta early in the morning in order to reach Hingalganj in the 24 Parganas district in good time. 'Canning' was the name of the last station. There, the tracks just ended. But the sea was still many miles off. Countless large and small tributaries of the river and several canals cut up the land. We were in the Ganges delta in Bengal. The atmosphere is always humid and sultry here, the earth constantly green and damp. Tall coconut palms sway in the breeze. The sun glitters and shimmers on the waves. Pretty motor-boats for passenger traffic and huge barges for heavy loads, narrow little fishing boats and junks with square sails enlivened the view. Our motor-boat rushed gaily through the water. The canal was about half a mile wide here. After a short while, we came across another canal, and then it seemed as if we were on the open sea. But it was only a 'crossing'; again we were in a canal. A village appeared – the friendly, reed-covered huts peeped from underneath the thick clusters of palm trees. Some people were waving from the bank for the boat to stop. A gang-plank was lowered. Women in gay apparel balanced on it with children riding on their hips and with large, wide baskets on their heads. Fishmongers brought their loads. Schoolchildren hopped in – for them this boat was the 'schoolbus'. In the distance we saw a little farmer running with fluttering garments. The boat hooted impatiently. Breathlessly, the little farmer came stumbling. In the distance we again discovered someone running. He, too, managed to come along. And then we saw yet another one running. . . . The boatman began to curse softly into his beard. But he waited. When he had finally pushed off but discovered another family with a large number

of children shouting and waving and giving him to understand that they, too, wanted to come along, he turned back
and landed a second time. It was a delight to sail through the
glittering splendour, on both sides the coconut groves and the
lovely villages. The sun set in a symphony of red and gold and
blue. We had reached the terminus of this boat. We now had
to traverse smaller channels and needed smaller boats. The
people from 'our' village had been waiting for us. A band
complete with drums and rattles struck up; we were given
garlands of flowers, speeches, fruits and tea. Then we were
put into a small, narrow fishing boat. More and more people
got into it, until it barely kept above water level, so much so,
in fact, that even the villagers had some misgivings. The
channels abound in sharks and a special kind of rather nasty
crocodile. It took some time to convince the occupants of
the boat that not all of them would be able to come along.
Finally, the boat lay sufficiently above water level. The channels
narrowed down and became more numerous. A silvery moon
was mirrored in the black waters; to left and right stood the
sharply cut silhouettes of the coconut palms; long-drawn cries
of water fowl were the only sound accompanying the clapping
of the oars and the rustle of the water.

It is like a journey through a fairy landscape. Suddenly,
our oarsman points to one side. A tiger island, he remarks.
The famous tigers of Bengal are now limited to some of these
delta islands – the channels are too broad for them, and so the
other islands are safe. Hour after hour we sailed through the
dark waters – the moon climbed higher and higher in the night
sky. On both sides, the banks were glistening, the water
flowed towards the sea. Another turning, and we saw bright
lamps on the embankment. The oarsman called out loudly –
at once there came a sound of drums and bells from the bank.
It was almost midnight, but the whole village had waited for

us. They all sang and clapped their hands – the drums rolled and the small, portable harmonium ground out the tune to which everybody danced. Again garlands, speeches, sweets. We were then supposed to partake of a festive meal. However, I wished to change my clothes, which had become soiled with mud, and the hosts crowding in the room agreed. It took some time to convince them that I did not need any spectators when changing. They left the room reluctantly, only to pile up around the windows. They poked their noses through the grills, trying to see what I would do. They were still there when I climbed into bed. Several times they lit up the room from the outside with a petromax lamp, probably whenever they wanted to satisfy the curiosity of a newly arrived visitor from another village who had not yet seen me.

Next morning, before sunrise, began the festivities proper for the Swami's birthday. A group of men arrived, dancing and singing, with bells and a small portable harmonium – they call it Nagara Kirtan. They continued to dance and sing in front of the house in which we were lodged. They decorated the celebrant with garlands and then left, singing and dancing. The whole day long, people came – some of them had even crossed the canal that marks the border with Pakistan, without papers and at great risk to their lives.

A big festive meal was planned for lunch. The villagers and friends of the Swami had subscribed to rice, vegetables and sweets; they had been cooking and preparing for days. Giant cauldrons steamed above fire holes that looked like young volcanoes. Two thousand people would be fed in the Swami's honour. Long before the meal was ready, the children were present in droves. They checked on what was being cooked, helped a little, swept the floor and fetched water. In return they got the first tit-bits.

At twelve sharp the bells and drums began to sound in

front of Swami Sangha's little temple, where the festivities took place. To the jingling of bells, the sound of drums, the recitation of bhajans and strange, shrill cries from the women, four nicely decorated brass dishes were brought with the God's meal: every day Krishna is served first, in the temple as well as in the homes. He really does get it, inasmuch as he is really present in his murti. This 'prayer before meals' lasts for about fifteen minutes. After this ritual, the first group of guests sat down. They sat facing each other in two parallel rows, on the floor of course, cross-legged, as is their custom. Each one was handed a clean banana leaf for a plate. First, it was sprinkled with water, then, a short mantra was recited, and then came the first course: out of a huge bucket a helping of rice was tilted on to the banana leaf. The rice was festively cooked with cinnamon, raisins and saffron. Then came a row of large brass buckets filled with various kinds of vegetables, dal and curry. Naturally, the food was strictly vegetarian, but unbelievably good. Indian cooks – if they are good – have a masterly way of handling spices and produce the most interesting dishes. As always, water was drunk from metal goblets. In the delta area all water tastes slightly brackish and salty, because of the proximity of the sea. There are, of course, no springs. Only the wealthy can afford to drink the milk of coconuts instead of water; it is somewhat sweetish, with a slight coconut flavour. A real refreshment, especially when all other drinks have a salty taste.

The meal lasted for several hours. Not that everybody was eating for that length of time: new shifts of eaters arrived constantly. They changed over every half-hour, during which most of the people devoured a surprisingly large amount of food. For the last shift, towards four o'clock, some who had been at the first session turned up again. . . .

In the afternoon, the intelligentsia arrived – the teachers, schoolmasters, pandits and petty officials of the neighbourhood. Their questions were interesting, at least for a farming village. In Europe, it would be extremely difficult to find a village where, earnestly and with genuine interest, questions such as these would be discussed: Does God have a shape or not? Is there only one Saviour or are there several? Does one earn grace or is it only obtainable as a gift? Certainly, these are questions belonging to the classical repertory of Indian philosophical discussions; but it is remarkable with what persistence and competence these questions are discussed. Hour after hour we sat, talking, discussing; occasionally one or the other would intersperse a harmless joke. Some came, some went. The children were especially eager. They were instructed by their elders to prostrate themselves before the Swami and to touch his feet. The little boys did this with élan. They threw themselves flat on their bellies, sprawling. Adults did it somewhat more gracefully; they always left a large bank-note at the Swami's feet.

Every evening, there was a large gathering in one of the villages of the neighbourhood, and we would be taken there. Everywhere, preparations had been going on for days. Young banana trees had been cut to decorate entrance portals. Garlands of flowers were in abundance. A large dais with a tent roof was set up for the celebrities. For weeks before, printed invitations had been circulated and all local newspapers had publicized our arrival on a big scale. The celebrations usually lasted till the small hours of the morning. But the many thousands who had come endured it. Naturally, I, too, had to speak – about Christ. Out of compassion for the people, who had already listened to so many lengthy speeches and sermons about Krishna and Radha, I thought it a good idea to be brief and contented myself with twenty minutes. It is impossible to say whether the people were listening. It always looked as if their eyes were glued to the speaker's lips. After me, another Vaishnava spoke. He took up one of the expressions of Jesus that I had quoted: 'Father, forgive them, for they know not what they do', and discoursed on it for an hour. While he was speaking, one of the organizers came up to me and said that my speech had been far too short; the people expected that I would talk for at least an hour. So I had to speak for a second time, for one hour. It is not difficult to find a subject for discussion here: a religious theme is always welcome. So I told in detail of the life and work of Christ, about the meaning of Christian priesthood, about the church. My Swami repeated it in Bengali.

One evening, there was a celebration in my honour. Invitations had been printed in all the newspapers, and the time specified in the programme was 4.30 p.m. By 5.30 p.m. nobody had turned up. But carpets were being spread, microphones installed. Towards 7 o'clock it turned dark – and then they arrived. The square was filled to capacity. The lights functioned spasmodically; the microphone was in a good mood. The organizer was absolutely hoarse. He had ruined his voice during the preparations. We moved to the dais in a solemn procession. Wreaths of flowers, garlands, more and more bouquets – the sound of drums and harmonium and bells. Then talks, countless speeches. One by me, of course. Everybody who within a radius of fifty miles had any name and rank gave a speech. Then, the welcoming speeches were read off: in Bengali and English. The texts were already printed and framed; after reading them, one was handed over to me as a souvenir.

'Oh, the great saint of the East and West,' it began, 'today on the occasion of your gracious arrival at this humble village of ours, we, the inhabitants of Hingalganj, beg to offer our warmest and heartfelt felicitations. May you be graced with

greater and greater glories in furthering the all-round development of our ideas and in preaching the message of merciful
Lord, the creator of this universe! The great yearning of
divine realization has overpowered your mind and you have
decided to dedicate your life to the cause of suffering humanity.
The fascinating life and teachings of Sri Chaitanya captivated
your mind and you decided to expose to the people his noble
and universal ideas of love and sacrifice. You are a sincere
advocate of truth and do not hesitate to forgo the most
cherished ideas if you find it necessary to do so in the search for
universal truth. You have renounced these worldly affairs of
common people and withdrawn yourself for the great service
of humanity by uplifting them from this narrow environment.
You are truly worthy of expressing the innermost essence of the
voice of the soul of India. You can deliver her people from the
influence of the war-thirsty spirit of the Devil. You have been
rendering services of boundless welfare to the people of East
and West by propagating the holy message of the religion of
love. May you live long for the spiritual uplift of humanity at
large!'

In a second welcoming speech, which followed, my admirers
were told that I was born 'in Munich, in a pious family of
monks', and that, 'sanatana dharma, otherwise known as
Hindu religion, is eternal and self-revealed, not man-created
but God-given. It is the eternal religion of all ever existing
animate souls, distinct from physical and mental existence.'
The speech concluded with the blessing: 'May Lord Shri
Krishna, our Deliverer and Mentor, give you the long life
for the best service of the humanity at large.'

The gathering continued – bhajans, speeches, speeches,
bhajans. . . . A man of about eighty approached us. Some time
ago, he had suffered a stroke and was partly paralysed on his
right side. He asked me if my blessing would cure him. 'That

depends on God's will,' I told him. In any case, I should bless him. I did so. Then he went to the Swami to ask for his blessing, too. It was almost 2 a.m. when the meeting was over.

Next day, I had to go from house to house – they all wanted to feed me at least once. Most of the houses belonged to small-holders: an acre or two on the average. The soil is good, the climate tropical – one doesn't need much. But even this small piece of land is not worked by the proprietor. He engages a servant and sits around the house. It isn't surprising that even in these distant, pious villages there are so many who vote communist at the elections.

The parting was moving. A crowd accompanied me to the boat on which I was to return to Calcutta. The voyage was equally beautiful and untroubled: bright sunshine, glittering water, gay colours. And yet I had grown more pensive, my thoughts were not so much concerned with the beauty of the landscape. What had happened during those days? It had all been pleasant and beautiful, apparently. But I had begun to understand several things. I compared the journey with the Swami with a similar one made together with a Catholic missionary through the villages of central India, the previous year. Which was more 'genuine'? How far has the church in India been able to appeal to the people and convince them?

The return trip in the train was similar to the journey there. Overcrowded compartments. At least I managed to get a seat for the thirty hours ahead of me. A family with eight children had occupied the floor of one of the compartments and made it their dormitory. Towards morning, the people tried, one by one, to squeeze themselves through to the washroom. The children were sleeping. One of the men seemed drowsy. With his shoe he stepped right onto the face of one of the children, unintentionally, of course. The mother began to rail at him and to belabour him with her fists. The man was somewhat embarrassed. The atmosphere was against him. He pulled his purse. He took out the key of his suitcase, in order to fetch his toilet things, and disappeared. The little boy's face had swollen up in the meantime; blood ran from his nose and mouth. The man returned from the washroom, clean-shaven and in a good mood. He was vexed because the little boy had taken his window seat while he had been away.

At the junction, I had to wait for a connection to Vrindaban. I went to the Catholic parish. When I told the Father there where I had been, he laughed at me. Nobody came to him to speak about religion – he was only approached for milk powder, oil and flour, gifts from American Catholics. Nobody asked whether God's grace was free or had to be earned. In order to receive the tangible gifts from the missionary, one had to do what he said. 'You will not get far with your idealism,' he said, and perhaps he was right. I had never sent home any statistics of successes and baptisms. 'We are realists,' he said. 'Come and eat meat again, it will make you think more sensibly.'

Indian Christmas

Gopalji prepared for the birthday of his Lord and God. It was the seventh Krishnapaksha of the month Shravana in the year two thousand and twenty-one Vikram. Gopalji was seventy-four years old; his life was behind him. His wife had died many years ago, the children of his sons were already adults. He had no more wishes, no more claims. This feast remained the highlight of each year; since he had come here into the town where, many thousand years ago, his Lord and God was born a man, all his love belonged to him and to the memory of his glorious birth.

All day he had been fasting. Not a grain of rice, not a drop of water had passed his lips. It was hot and sultry – the monsoons had set in. The fields were already green, the foliage on the trees was thick and dark. Men and animals would again find nourishment and water, life-giving water. It was all the grace of the Lord – with his advent the world begins to bloom, with his arrival the blessings of heaven come upon the earth. The peacocks in the trees uttered their long-drawn, plaintive cries; they announced the rain. Blue-black clouds piled up in the sky.

'How beautiful is the Lord!' thought Gopalji while he was washing and dressing the small metal figure of the divine child. With great love he dressed it in the festive robe of yellow silk. He polished the artistic silver cradle with damp earth and soft rags. Then he lay the child on silken pillows. He put incense sticks into a holder and arranged the many little bowls and utensils necessary for the puja, the religious service.

It grew dark. Flashes of lightning pierced the evening sky. One after the other, the friends arrived who used to sing God's praises with him every day. They left their sandals at the entrance, prostrated themselves in front of the image of the Lord and then touched Gopalji's feet as a sign of respect. With crossed legs they sat on the carpet in front of the shrine. Softly, Gopalji started the first bhajan: 'Gopala gokula vallavi priya gopa gosuta vallabham. . . .' Most of those present began a rhythmic clapping of hands, one of them marking the timing with a dhol-drum. Several sounded cymbals, while the chanting remained restrained.

But after half an hour enthusiasm rose in the small community. The singing grew loud, the accompanying instruments boomed and clinked; here one of them would suddenly exclaim a loud 'Jai Krishna', another would get up and begin to dance and sit down again, a third one would give a sharp beat on the cymbals. Outside, a raging thunderstorm broke out. Although the windows were small, the room was almost incessantly lit by lightning. In the blue-white light one could see how the storm seized the trees and pressed them down, how the rain rushed down in sheets and little torrents rolled through the narrow lanes. But what did it matter?

The rain slackened, the flashes of lightning seemed more distant, only a continuous muffled rolling lay in the air. It was almost midnight. Gopalji picked up the holy book from which he read daily and where he found all the wisdom and piety, philosophy and rules of life. 'When the auspicious hour of grace had struck, the heavens cleared, the firmament was radiant with countless stars: the whole world, the cities and the villages were in festive attire, the rivers were full of clear water, the lotus flowers adorned the pools with shining beauty, the trees of the forests bloomed, everything was enchanted by the sweet song of birds and the humming of bees. A gentle breeze brought sweet fragrance. The sacred fires flamed up. The minds of the pious, so long oppressed by evil spirits and demons, were gladdened. When the unborn Lord was born, drums boomed in the sky, the heavenly choirs sang and played, the elves and nymphs danced for joy. In a delightful shower the heavenly flower petals fell down, the clouds rolled gently like the waves of the sea. When it was midnight, in impenetrable darkness, the Lord who lives in every heart revealed himself through Devaki, who resembled a heavenly one, like the full moon in the Eastern sky. The child illuminated the room with his splendour; thus Vasudeva, the foster father of Krishna, was certain that it was Lord Vishnu in person, and he made ready to bow down low and praise him with a pure mind and with folded hands: "You, Lord, have revealed yourself physically to me, you who are the most high, beyond all things material, full of bliss and unique, all-knower. Although you are within things, you cannot be recognized through them. In you, there is no exterior and no interior. You are in all, and all is in you. In you there are beginning, existence and end of this creation. With the intention of protecting this world, O Lord and ruler, you descended into my house." ' His voice shaking with emotion, Gopalji had read thus far; now he broke into sobs and wept for joy over the birth of the Lord. He passed the book on to the person sitting next to him, so that he might finish the solemn report of the birth of the Lord. 'Devaki, who saw her child distinguished with the marks of Vishnu, smiled at him and praised him: "You are the Lord Vishnu, the enlightenment of all living beings, the ineffable reality, the absolute essence, free of every blot of activity. When in the fullness of time the universe dissolves and the elements pass away, then you alone remain in existence. Time is only one of your manifestations. I take refuge in you, the ruler and protector. In fear of the snake of death, rushed hither and thither in this world, man can find no place where he may live without fear. But as soon as he has reached your lotus feet, O Eternal One, he rests in peace. Protect us who are in fear. You dispel the fear of your servants. Do not reveal to the ignorant this divine form, the object of highest meditation." Thus spoke Devaki. Then the Lord opened his mouth and said: "Always think of me as your son and also as the Most High – thus you will always be united with me most intimately." Then the Lord was silent and at once took on the form of an ordinary child. His parents were amazed at this miracle.'

No sooner had the last word been read than the drums, the bells and the cymbals began to sound; the women uttered shrill cries, the men got up; sobbing and weeping they began to dance. One cried 'Hari Krishnaaa!' as loudly as he could, the others joined in. From the neighbouring houses and from the temples, loud calling and ringing of bells could be heard. Gopalji pulled the curtain that had hidden the divine child; he lit the lights and incense sticks and began the most solemn puja of the whole year. One after the other each prostrated himself before the image of God and touched it reverently.

The meal had already been prepared the previous day. First it was set before the Lord, before him who creates everything and preserves and absorbs everything into himself. Whatever man eats, is his prasad, his gift of grace. It was the most festive and the gayest meal of the year. It was not for nothing that they had fasted the whole day. Mountains of chapatis and large quantities of rice disappeared. Each person had twelve little brass bowls in front of him, containing the ingredients: all kinds of vegetables with various spices, sweet things and sour things, entrées and desserts. More was served constantly, water was poured, and everyone praised the food. Loud and easy belching indicated that the guests were satisfied. They washed hands and mouths and took leave with folded hands: 'Namaskar' – 'Radhe Shyam'. And now I was alone with Gopalji.

It was early morning, the stars paled. Gopalji was happy. 'Only one wish I have left in my life,' he began; 'I would like to see the Lord in the body, just as Vasudeva and Devaki saw him. When I was a boy, one day a holy man came into the house of my father. He told me much about the saints who had been honoured by seeing Lord Krishna – by having sakshatkar. He took my hand and prophesied that I, too, would see him.' Lost in thought, he moved the cymbals and sang softly to himself: 'Govind tum saranai main aya . . . I wait only for him. In my dream I have seen him already – deep blue, radiant, with four arms, with discus, shell, club and bow, with the peacock feather in his hair and the Kaustubha jewel on his breast – he was beautiful beyond description. For weeks on end, I was beside myself with happiness after this dream. But I want to see him in reality, serve him eternally in Vaikuntha.'

'Have you ever seen Jesus Christ before you?' he suddenly asked me. 'Has he never appeared to you, not even in a dream?'

'No,' I said, 'never.'

'Do you think he could appear to you – just as he appeared to Peter and John after the resurrection? Can't you see him in the Eucharist?'

I had known Gopalji long enough not to be surprised by his questioning. One of his teachers, a devout Hindu, had been the first to tell him of Christ in school, and had given him a copy of the First Gospel. Gopalji was convinced that God had appeared in Christ. 'I adore the divinity of Christ,' he had told me already months ago; 'but I also adore the divinity of

Shri Krishna.' God has appeared at different times and in different places on earth, to save the good and punish the wicked. He will come again as a rider on a white horse, as Kalkin, to destroy finally all the wickedness of the world.

It had become day. Between large clouds, a radiantly blue sky, a glaring sun. The people went in gay small groups to the temple. Loudspeakers poured out the recitation of the history of the birth of Krishna according to the Bhagavata Purana. A rich merchant had donated the money, in order to gain blessings for himself and the town. Children in new, colourful clothes, sat in front of the houses, with small cradles, in which they rocked the child Krishna.

'Tell me about the birth of God as Jesus Christ,' Gopalji begged of me. 'Let me understand Jesus the way you understand him, let me see his heart.'

He gave me the gospels – he read them daily. 'In those days it came to pass that the emperor Augustus issued an edict. . . .' In his mind, Gopalji had often contemplated the scene – Joseph and Mary and the child, the shepherd and the entire landscape. With folded hands he said: 'Peace to God on high and on earth peace among men . . . Om, shanti, shanti, ohm.' He knew the texts by heart.

I began to tell him what Christmas meant for those of us who grow up as Christians. The festive midnight services, the stars and bells, the Christmas tree and the lights. I told him of all the Christmas celebrations I could remember. Of the children who wait for little Jesus and are happy about the toys, cakes and candles. I told him of Christmas in war-time, the Holy Night in the air raid shelter, of Christmas during the evacuation, of Christmas in the forest with the boy scouts, of the secret preparing and buying of gifts in order to make someone happy, of the rich man's Christmas and the Christmas of the poor. I told him about Christmas in Munich and the 'Christkindlmarkt', the Christmas bazaar, of Christmas in Rome with the shepherds from the Abruzzi mountains playing their bagpipes, of Christmas in Vienna with the large choirs and orchestras in the churches, of Christmas in Bombay with balloons and paper garlands and the five-pronged stars wishing everyone a 'Merry Xmas', of Christmas in Mathura and the young men from Bihar who, after midnight service, danced their folk-dances around the church the whole night through. I tried to make him feel how, each year, the enchantment of Christmas makes people kinder and more helpful, how the memory of God becoming man makes people grow more human, how it reveals their good-will and their kind heart, how Christ has the power, even today, to move hearts.

Gopalji had listened with interest. 'The Lord comes for the delight of the good. The wicked do not even see him. He is mysterious – he wants to serve us and to be served by us. He wants to be our child and friend and playmate and husband. He wants to jest with us and play, like a small child. . . .' He laughed aloud. On the road we could see a man shouting and abusing. With one hand he held his head, with the other one he tried to retrieve the end of his turban which was dangling high above him. A little monkey, the kind that hop around by the hundreds here in town, had grabbed the headgear of the villager with a daring sweep. With both hands he pulled it. Half a dozen little Hanumans watched with interest. The smallest ones clung to their mothers. 'God has a very good sense of humour,' said Gopalji, still laughing. 'Jestingly, he wants to rid us of all that is superfluous.' The man with the turban was still scolding. Without his turban. Half a dozen monkeys amused themselves with the long, bright red strip of cloth, they wrapped themselves in it, rolled one another about and screeched with delight. Lastly, they let it flutter from a branch. 'Would the silly man quarrel with the monkey if he thought that Krishna was wanting to play with his turban?' Gopalji interjected. 'Everything is his play, his lila. If only people could see that he is in everything, that everything proceeds from him, sickness and health, life and death, the turban and the monkey – would they still grieve or get agitated? Men do not recognize him, although he is everywhere. They are misled by their own covetousness. But why talk about it? Let us meditate on the mystery of the birth of the Unborn, who is born in many forms.'

'In the beginning was the Word, and the Word was with God, and God was the Word . . .'

'Om . . ,' said Gopalji. 'He is the mysterious mantra, the Word existing from eternity, the name of God who was given to men as the safest means for crossing the ocean of this transitoriness. In God's name is all power and grace – He purifies us . . .'

Gopalji listened carefully when I told of the eternal birth of the Son from the Father. That, too, was not new to him.

'Ram nam satya hai, Ram nam satya hai . . .' – it came upon us in a monotonous rhythm. One of the many processions to the burning ghats. 'Ram nam satya hai . . .' The name of God is truth. The people believe that they reach God immediately if they pronounce his name at the last moment and invoke him in their mind. 'Ram nam satya hai . . .' It faded into the distance.

'Do you think we will be together in eternity?' Gopalji asked me. 'Would you consider me a Christian, as I am?'

'Love God with all your heart and with all your power and your neighbour as yourself,' Christ had replied to one who wanted to know the meaning of 'Christianity'. Gopalji loved God in the way he understood him – he employed all his time and strength to serve him, to know him better. Every instant his name was on his lips; ceaselessly the mala, a kind of rosary, moved through his fingers – each bead an invocation of the name of God. He was good to all who came to him. He possessed nothing beyond the few trifles in this room. He tried to incorporate the teachings of his Mahaprabhu, his 'Great Lord' – to be humbler than a blade of grass, more patient than a tree, and to praise God always. On many a day he fasted completely. He had no enemy. 'I am the door,' Christ had said; 'all who came before me were thieves and robbers.' Was the one who had taught him to regard everything as lila, as the play of a loving God, a thief and a robber? I wonder if he did not venerate Christ in Krishna – and Krishna within Christ? Was he not closer to the mystery of God and his incarnation than many who call themselves Christians? Was it not Christ who united us in friendship, who had brought us together here on Krishna's birthday to speak of his birth?

What does it mean to be a Christian? We have a small verse from one of our poet-mystics: 'And if Christ was born a thousand times in Bethlehem and not within you, you would be lost eternally.' Christ must be born in each one of us. Gopalji was already 'reborn', a dvijati – he had received the samnyasi-initiation, was dead to the world. What more was necessary?

Would he see Christ in the flesh as God, if he were baptized? No – it was a matter of other depths: faith, communion with God, love.

'Gopalji,' I asked. 'Have you never doubted Krishna?'

'Yes,' he replied. 'As a young man I have doubted. I found everything so childish and unscientific and boring. But my guruji, my religious teacher, opened my eyes to reality. And since then I have never again doubted God – only men and the world. I have begun to understand that he is reality, that our so-called science remains on the surface, that he lives in the innermost of our heart, where no human science penetrates. It is because of grace that we recognize him. Doubt is the worst kind of poison for the man who seeks God. He must believe, believe with all his heart, even if all the other people take him for a madman, just as they thought Chaitanya and Mira Bai and Ramakrishna – those great saints – mad. They were not insane – the world was insane. They were within reality, the world is unreal. God is everywhere, but men are blind.'

'Gopalji,' I asked. 'Is it not presumptuous to choose one's own Ishtadevata, the God one adores?'

'It is not we who choose our God, it is God who chooses us,' he replied. 'It is in his power to attract or repel us, to let us do good or evil. We cannot do anything on our own. But even when he destroys us, it is for our salvation, if only we see that it is he. But human beings forget so easily. Today they celebrate his birth – tomorrow they have forgotten him. Sometimes I am so filled with nausea that I call for him with tears in my eyes.'

'Is he not continuously arriving?' I interjected. 'Even in the people of goodwill who proclaim his peace? He has told us to proclaim his kingdom – to live in the expectation of his arrival. He is still being born out of God and within human beings who welcome the word of God.'

'Yes,' said Gopalji, 'he is still being born.' For a long while he contemplated the child Krishna and hummed a little bhajan to himself. 'Yes, there are good people even today; but they are not the loud ones who speak over the wireless, not the famous ones, who have ministers taking part in their pious kirtan singing. They are the quiet and patient ones – they are the salt of the earth. God visits them and in them he comes to us. Do you know the story of Daridranara Narayana? God took on the shape of a poor man. He went to the richest man in the village and asked for food and shelter for the night. But that one chased him away. He went to the poorest man

who lived outside the village. This one welcomed him honour-
ably and shared his poor meal and his miserable hut with him.
When God asked what reward he wished to have, he replied
that he wished to serve God. Has not God been born within
the poor man?'

It was still Janmashtami, Krishna's birthday. On a pony cart,
the festively attired boys passed by with solemn demeanour.
They would, in the evening, perform the Raslila, the play of
Krishna with the gopis; the play of God with humankind,
type and fulfilment of human life. Gopalji wanted to know
whether we, too, played God's lila during Christmas. Yes, we,
too, play God's lila – with flutes and violins and choirs, in the
paintings and sculptures of great masters, in the fervent representations of folk art. Even India already has her Indian
Christmas plays – her Christmas songs and dances expressing
the joy over his arrival. 'The joy over his arrival,' Gopalji
repeated pensively. 'Is it not the only real joy we have? Everything is transitory – everything dies. Only he does not die and
those who know him. I do not long for riches or fame – I
only long for him. Master Narada, the author of the bhakti-
sutras, says that the love a lover feels when he is separated
from his loved one is the highest kind of love. Sometimes I
think I am unable to bear the pain of separation any longer.
Perhaps we have to sink even deeper into ignorance, to come
away from him even further, feel the pain of separation even
more sharply, before he comes.'

Gopalji was silent. For minutes, not a word was said. But
we both knew that we were thinking of the same thing: of
him and of his coming.

And when he comes, what will be? Will men recognize him
this time and accept him? Will they really love him? Will he
not, once again, shame the wisdom of the scribes, once again
upset the tables of moneychangers in the temple, once again

disappoint the hopes of the politicians? Will he not again be crucified and buried – and forgotten?

'He *has* come,' said Gopalji. 'We must look for him. He only hides so that our impatience may grow and our love be purified – that we do not seek our pleasure, but his. He does not come to ease our life on earth – he comes out of his divine will, to teach us his love.'

A neighbour dropped in. He seated himself near us. A few more arrived. It was time for the daily bhajan. I left Gopalji and went home. The peacocks complained again. The frogs quacked contentedly in the large puddles created by the rain. The vultures sat peevishly and watchfully on their tree. They were awaiting daylight.

I began with Mass. Alone, in my poor room. The bells pealed from the nearby temple, bells rung by the people as they enter the temple. From nearby houses I could hear the bhajans, the rolling of dhols and the jingling of bells. Pilgrims passed by my window – 'Hare Krishna, Krishna Hare . . . ' Introit, Kyrie – the temple bells mixed with the Gloria. The prayer was accompanied by the kirtan. And the gospel told of the transfiguration of the Lord – 'do not tell anyone of it before the Son of man has risen from the dead'. Gopalji was in my mind; he would be speaking now in front of his small community about the advent of God, his advent in Gokula and in Bethlehem, in the hearts of men. He would try to interpret to his friends the mystery of the eternal birth of the Word from the Father – and again he would be so moved as to burst into sobs and tears, because he could not bear it that he was unable to see the Lord. Did I not also offer his pain and his longing on the paten? Was the wine not also the expression of his love? And did not Christ also transform Gopalji's miserable humanness into his own humanity, into his love for the Father? Would he not also take part in my communion with Christ? Was he not united with me, with Him?

It was August 6th, 1963 – but no Christmas has made me understand better the mystery of the coming of God, no Christmas has awakened within me a more urgent longing. And no Christmas will pass without the presence, in my mind, of Gopalji, of his love for his Lord, his longing, his questions. Nor shall I forget the peacocks, the frogs, the monkeys and the vultures, nor the lightning and the rushing water. But more than anything else I shall carry this with me as my Christmas mystery: that God gives to a man so much longing for his coming.

Everyday dialogue

Everyday life is in many respects the same everywhere – one meets good people and not so good ones, friendly and unfriendly ones, some that are diligent and others that are lazy, fat ones and thin ones, gay people and sad people, honest ones and dishonest ones, the pious and the pharisees, mockers and fanatics, people who are to be taken seriously and others whose thinking is confused, silent ones and gossips.

Everyday, a number of people would come to our institution; some were friends, others were simply curious and some were looking for shelter.

One day, a saffron-clad swami from Kerala asked for a night's shelter. He did not belong to any particular group; he had travelled far and wide, and held lectures in Germany and had even visited Padre Pio. With inimitably bland arrogance he spoke of the 'Catholic sects', and he knew that only the Carthusians practised meditation. He was interested in Therese von Konnersreuth and wanted to know my opinion of Padre Pio. I could only tell him what I had heard from others. Swamiji thought that everything was only fraud and trickery . . .

A devout old man lived in the same building. He took part every day in the temple puja and venerated people like Emerson, Paul Brunton and Vinoba Bhave. He was busy translating Emerson into Punjabi and came every ten minutes to ask for my interpretation of a Latin, Greek, French or Italian quotation.

He came to me after I had held a lecture on Christianity, to borrow a New Testament. He copied the Sermon of the Mount in his delicate handwriting and soon knew it by heart. A Hindu sadhu had recommended the *Imitation of Christ* to him. He now came to me every day, in order to read a chapter from it and to discuss it. In return he taught me a few verses of Kabir each day and I had to preach him a little 'sermon'. On my return from my yearly retreat in Agra he wanted to know what special enlightenment I had had. In some things he was odd; thus, he insisted for instance that it was his religious duty to walk six miles a day. He had measured a certain distance for this purpose and marched up and down this distance twenty times a day. But he was a kind man at heart, who was unable to hurt anyone and helped anyone he could. One day, he came with a surprise. He had heard that Catholics confess their sins to a priest and receive absolution. He wanted to confess to me. I felt pretty helpless. I listened to what he wished to say and gave him my blessing. He seemed visibly relieved. Once, when he saw me celebrate Mass, he was moved to tears. If he had a quarrel with anyone, he always tried to make it up and to ask forgiveness. For him, religion was life and life religion.

By four o'clock in the morning, Mangal Prabhu had begun his bhajan. He spent his life's evening as a sadhu in Vrindaban and was occupied almost the whole day with reading from the Bhagavatam Purana. He always greeted me in a friendly fashion and told everyone that I was 'pukka sadhu' – a real monk: the highest praise he had to bestow.

One evening, an old man in the yellow robe asked for food. Next morning he asked for work. He said he was a shorthand typist and that he had been in Calcutta, secretary to a well-known lawyer. At the end of his resources, he had only donned a monk's robe for the free train ride it involved. He had spent some time in Ayodhya and had turned Rama-bhakta. He told his life's story often and openly. His wife had chased him from the house because he did not earn enough money, drank too much and lived with bad girls. He had ruined himself physically and was glad to find a job with us. He could not sit behind his typewriter for more than ten minutes. He had a redeeming idea: the typewriter needed repairs. That helped for three weeks. Then the misery began all over again. They wanted to send him away, and he came to pour out his troubles to me. Would the church give him a good job if he got baptized and became a Christian? He asked me to baptize him; he was prepared to learn. He came more and more often and told me more and more details of his bungled life. Before he was dismissed, he came once more. He told me to be careful – on the open field in front of the house a ghost with a long arm was constantly trying to reach inside. He told me I should keep the light burning in my room throughout the night, then the ghost could not harm me.

Having no servants, I did my own shopping in the bazaar. I got talking to many people there. On the open road, someone will stop you and ask all sorts of questions; one hears extempore sermons on this and that subject as well as the latest news. A fantastically painted sadhu steered towards me. Did I know that Swami Shivananda of Rishikesh had died? No, I did not. I, too, had known Shivananda. Next morning he came to visit me. It was during the border incidents with China. I was to give him a letter of recommendation to Pandit Nehru and President Radhakrishnan. I doubted the success of such letters and asked him what he wanted with them. He said he had developed an infallible plan for the expulsion of the Chinese. His tremendous yoga-powers were sufficient to rule over the whole Himalayas. He attached only one small condition to the use of the tapas: he would have to be made Field Marshal. Another sadhu asked me, on the road, for help against police and robbers – both sides harassed him, he said. I wanted to know more clearly what his troubles were. He told me that the robbers as well as the police were constantly trying to enter his innermost being and create trouble there.

An aged neighbour, eighty-five years old and bearing his years well, had, in his old age, joined a swami who was known to be a realized soul. He spent every day, eighteen hours without interruption, in the contemplation of Krishna's love-play with the gopis – quite an art if one considers that Krishna has to be endowed with ever fresh ideas. The old neighbour came over almost every day for a chat, to talk about other people. So we learnt much of what was happening – and others heard of what went on with us. He often brought me a mango, an orange or some other ripe fruit. He had taken to the young Christian sadhu, so he said. One warm afternoon, he came to me. After the customary questions about health and well-being he showed me a small box wherein lay a not-so-new wrist watch. Did I want it? No, I already had one. Was it a good watch – what was its value? Naturally, I had no idea. Then came the beginning of the story.

From the days of his life in the world he had salvaged four hundred rupees for his religious life. His guru learnt of this and told him, if he, as a samnyasi, possessed so much money, he would end up in one of the worst hells and would then be reborn as a dog who eats his own vomit. This our pious neighbour did not want, of course – why had he left the world, after all? He spent all his money on this watch. The dealer had cheated him, moreover. Now he needed some clothing and had no money for it. He asked me to give him whatever I wanted for the watch. He also wished to know from me whether he would have gone to hell had he kept the money.

Bankey Biharji is the author of several books on mystics and bhaktas and an expert on sufism. He has also already translated several works from the Persian. He had once been an advocate and, still young, settled in Vrindaban, never to leave it again. He told me that the combination of Krishna-bhakti and sufism had come to him quite naturally. The Bhagavadgita was, for him, the book of books. He had a good library, and among his books were the complete works of the great Spanish mystics. He asked me about Therese von Konnersreuth. Twice a day, a small community meets at his house for satsang. Verses of the well-known bhakti poets are sung. A chapter of the Gita is recited daily, and in the end comes the beautiful, melancholy, pessimistic Bhaja Govindam of Shankara. Our postman was a regular participant at these satsangs, and he thought it edifying that I was there occasionally on a Sunday. 'We find time for so many other things,' he opined, 'we should also find a little time each day for God.' Bankey Biharji holds a little speech each time. He speaks of the well-known bhaktas, whose stories the people have known since childhood; he tells the Krishna stories, interprets the parables of the New Testament and quotes from the works of the sufis. He also speaks on Christian saints: Francis of Assisi, Theresa of Avila, John of the Cross, the monks Antony and Paphnutius. He declared himself to be a 'fakir' and would not accept pupils. He had a companion, Mata Krishnaji. As a young girl she had taken part in his daily satsang and wanted to join him for ever. To the despair of her father she refused all marriage proposals. Bankey Biharji accepted her as Mata Krishna – simultaneously as her guru and 'chela'. Both wore the pink monks' robes, and occasionally they could be seen out together. He showed me letters from girls in Sweden and Switzerland, who had had visions of Krishna and wished to come and join him. Bankey Biharji had written to them not to come – there was no genuine spirituality in India today. One day he asked me whether in Europe there still were contemplative orders of the kind founded by Theresa of Avila. I told him what I knew of the contemplative monastic orders. Mata Krishnaji proposed the founding of a contemplative order in the neighbourhood of Vrindaban, with the rules of Theresa of Avila. They wanted contemplation, not exhibition and religious busy-ness.

A student came every day to practise Hindi conversation with me. He came from a small village near Agra. Dacoits had killed both his parents when he was still very small; so he grew up with his uncle here in Vrindaban. The uncle was a sadhu, and Prem himself was a pious young man doing his daily devotion in front of Krishna and building small altars. One day we spoke of Krishna. 'Well,' I said; 'if you did all the things Krishna did – steal butter and milk, hide the clothes of girls bathing – you would hardly be thought to be a good boy.'

'Yes,' he replied, 'Krishna is bad; but he is Krishna, he can afford it.'

Wasn't it irreverent the way they treated Krishna? They tease him, they mock him, make a fool of him!

'No,' said the boy. 'He wants it here, it is possible only in Vrindaban. Elsewhere it would be wrong—here, it is correct.'

One day, he came to me with a handful of question papers. He had seen a Bible course advertised in the newspaper, promising a final diploma. He received the New Testament in small brochures regularly and had to return the completed question papers. He asked me to check his answers. I wanted to know how he liked the gospels. Most of it he did not understand, he said. It wasn't Hindi. It was Hindi all right, but not the language he found in his own religious books. And then, there were many foreign words that were not explained sufficiently. Did the Christian religion interest him? No, he only wanted the diploma. And the Bible was free of charge. Prem is friendly, clean and ready to help; he fasts strictly on all Vaishnava fasting days and has been given the nickname 'Babaji' by his fellow-pupils, which roughly means 'little monk'.

A starving old Brahmin came, with nothing but a tiny shred of cloth between his legs. He said he had been expelled from his family and would do any kind of work in return for food. Although no one was needed, he was allowed to wash the dishes and sweep the rooms. He did it thoroughly: the plates he licked clean with his tongue and rinsed them afterwards. While doing so, he continuously murmured to himself: 'These here are mlecchas, and I am a Brahmin. But now I am a servant, a servant. . . .' Although he had also been given a plate, he preferred to eat from a rusty tin, together with the dogs. He could never get enough and scraped the remnants off our plates. When he had regained his strength, he quarrelled continuously with the cook. He abused him in the foulest terms and threw at him whatever he could lay his hands on. When he came to my room, he prostrated himself fully in front of the crucifix. Occasionally he would stand in front of it for a few minutes, arms outstretched like the crucified one. He also wanted to bathe the cross every day, just like the Vaishnavas did with their murtis. One day, he brought a handful of blossoms and put them below the cross. It was September 14th, the feast of the elevation of the cross. He paid special respect to the cassock. If he saw one of my cassocks hanging in the room, he would bow before it and pin flowers to it. How many cassocks did I have? he wanted to know. He asked me to give him one. When a friend from another missionary society in Benares came to pay us a visit, the old man admired the cross on his chest. The next morning he had painted, instead of the Vaishnava symbols, three white crosses with gopicanda on chest and forehead. He said there were four kinds of people praying: some pray that God should preserve their wealth, others that God should give them wealth. Those who asked for heaven were better; but those who neither had nor wanted riches and did not ask for heaven, but only wished to serve God for his own sake, they were the best. One day he was sent away, after he had fought another lengthy skirmish with the cook.

One fine day, a few students who had come frequently in order to learn something about Europe brought an acquaintance of theirs – a businessman from Kanpur, extremely rich, as they said, and interested in Christianity. The first question was whether Christ had been a man or a woman. When I said 'a man', his interest cooled down considerably. He mistook a picture of the madonna with the child for a photograph of my wife. He did not want to believe that I was not married. If I was indeed still a bachelor, then I should marry a girl from Bengal. He knew a good, beautiful girl for me.

One of my colleagues was a distinguished professor emeritus of philosophy. He was already over seventy, but had a lively interest in philosophy and read with great zeal the latest books about Anglo-American linguistic analysis. He came almost daily to engage me in his private philosophical discussions. 'We seldom are of one opinion,' he smilingly told the vice-chancellor of the university during a visit, but I was the only one here, so he said, with whom it was a real pleasure for him to discuss philosophy. He recommended me to other colleagues and asked me for my co-operation in a comprehensive publication on philosophical themes. One of his students was to hold a seminar lecture on 'immortality'. He found it difficult and asked me for my help. Naturally, what

I prepared for him was not quite the opinion of the professor. On the afternoon of the seminar, he sent a messenger saying the student was not quite ready with his preparations. Then, the professor himself helped. The end result was, that one could say nothing on individual immortality, since one could not prove philosophically the existence of individuals. For weeks we continued our discussion privately; I do not know whether I managed to convince him that existence can only be experienced and not proved *a priori*.

One day, he asked me to hold a seminar on 'universal religion'. When, after a summary and critical analysis of various greater and lesser religions that think of themselves as universal, I began to quote a few essential texts from Paul in order to demonstrate why and in what sense Christianity understands itself as a 'universal religion', he became nervous and interrupted me continuously: 'I do not understand this, I do not understand this.' The discussion ended with the problem why the Aryans write from left to right and the Semites from right to left. A swami solved the problem: primitive humanity had lived in Persia and the Aryans migrated towards the right, the Semites to the left . . . .

A jovial, stout police official greeted me on the road with a loud 'buon giorno'. He stopped the rickshaw to speak to me. He told me how he took part in the Italian campaign and that he now was the police chief here. He enquired affably whether I could stand the constant vegetarian diet, whether I did not wish to hunt or fish; there was venison and fish to be had in the neighbourhood. I declined, explaining that I was for 'ahimsa', non-killing, and that I found the vegetarian diet excellent. Later I came to know that, a few years ago, he had hooked a European doctor in this manner: he invited him to hunt and told him after the deed was done that hunting was forbidden, and that he had now to pay a penalty of five thousand rupees.

A tall man in a saffron robe paid us a visit. He introduced himself as the 'Editor-in-Chief' of the 'Hindustan Forward' – 'A Local Intellectual's Publication', as the sub-title read. The 'Hindustan Forward' appears at irregular intervals and regularly publishes several photographs of the 'Editor-in-Chief' and a lengthy article about him praising him as the greatest speaker of this century, as a yogi and intellectual. Equally regularly appear the most massive invectives against the government, so vicious as to be unprintable. The 'Editor-in-Chief' wore the monk's robe, but he was married and lived with his wife and five children. He had been in Turkey as a preacher and introduced me now to the local Arya Samaj Gurukul, the 'seminary'. He recommended Savarkar's 'Hindutva' as the best book on Hinduism. Savarkar was the main ideologist of the Hindu Mahasabha, the most extreme radical Hindu group existing. He said that I should wear the Indian monk's robe, rather than the white one I was accustomed to – the people would 'adore' me. He wanted to introduce me to his kind of yoga and mentioned a string of several high-standing people who were learning from him. It was a kind of yoga I wanted to have nothing to do with; it is revolting even to speak or write of it. He knew hair-raising stories about the moral depravity of the Vaishnava swamis, each of whom – so he said – had several 'sadhinis', and he related how someone wanted to kill him because he had publicly said the truth about a famous swami. He also knew that there was a group of sadhus who, for five rupees, would take orders for committing any murder. He read a great future out of my palm and wanted twelve rupees as well as my photograph, in order to make propaganda for me in the 'Hindustan Forward'. I declined with thanks. . . .

These are the outward aspects of daily life in the dialogue. Study, which is most essential, requires a great deal of time and effort. It is definitely a harsher discipline than much of what is described in the old legends of saints' lives. One discovers no progress, no spiritual progress either. Yet it has to be done. If one sees only the surface, like certain tourists and journalists, then the whole of Hinduism could be dismissed as superstition and nonsense. But the surface is misleading; there is so much pure gold in the soil, once one begins to dig. And it is our task to unearth this gold. 'Dialogue' is not only the registering of each visible phenomenon; dialogue is creative in itself, it is a release. Only in the dialogue does a Hindu learn the essence of Hinduism, and the Christian find the essence of Christianity. Just as important as the 'external' dialogue, the encounter with the non-Christian in conversation, is the 'inner' dialogue, the debate with the essence of Hinduism in our own hearts. There the decisions are taken, there new insights are gained.

He who has understood the meaning of the dialogue will not want to have anything more to do with academic dalliance or a science of comparative religion, behaving as if it stood above all religions. He will also not want to know anything more of a certain kind of theology that works 'without presuppositions' and pleases itself in manipulating definitions and formulas and forgets about man, who is the main concern. He will be more and more pulled into what is called 'spirituality': the real life of the mind. I wanted to see a famous man in Benares, a sagacious philosopher, feared by many as a merciless critic of Christian theology. I had my own reasons for paying him a visit. He was polite, invited me for tea and then mounted the attack. I let him talk his fill, without saying a word myself. Then I started to talk about the things I had begun to understand within the dialogue – quite positively Christian. We got into a sincere, good, deep discussion. He had intended to send me away after ten minutes. When I left after two hours, he had tears in his eyes: 'If we insisted on our theologies – you as a Christian, I as a Hindu – we should be fighting each other. We have found one another because we probed more deeply, towards spirituality.'

9

Experiment in faith

Neither romanticism nor rashness, neither a crusader's spirit nor despair about Europe, but the fruit of much deliberation, years of study, numerous discussions, and, so he hoped, also a real vocation had impelled him to leave the West. Even the study of theology had not broken anything essential of this faith, and concrete practical experience with those who take themselves for direct representatives of God had only led him to decide in favour of the kingdom of God and grow critical in respect of men, especially when they come forward with totalitarian claims. The vague impression that, somehow, he was outside reality, and the senselessness of a large portion of the routine was merely due to the situation; reality was still to come. Or had it started already? He had few illusions – too few, according to the opinion of many. As a child, he had grown during the war and post-war periods and had seen already then that human beings can be very evil. And also very good.

He rejoiced when he first saw the temple towers of the town, where the real encounter was to happen to him; he was glad to see the orange-coloured sadhus, the monks with their kumbhas, the water vessels. He did not think much of comfort and the so-called standard of living and he did not mind at all, therefore, that most people were poor and that he would live just like those people.

His first Mass in his small room was also the first Mass that had ever been celebrated in this town. It was the sacred town of Krishna, and local law specifies that all missionary activity and the erection of any kind of Christian church would be punishable. No one before him had celebrated the Eucharist here, and it was likely that no one would celebrate with him, for a long time to come. He believed in the community of saints, independent of physical nearness. He thought of his friends, united with him in Christ. It was hot; he liked the heat and he was prepared to accept reality such as it was.

The outward happenings were hardly worth mentioning. Life in the small town went on as it probably had for centuries. The town lived for Krishna – Krishna was the main event here: his festivals, his ideas, his friends, his party. The great events of world politics did not touch him. Sometimes he was under the impression that this was a world totally different from the one he had grown up in – as if whatever he read in the newspapers about atom bombs and wars, of gigantic industry and political power-blocs, was only a product of his feverish imagination. For months on end he read no newspaper; the world here was easier to understand if one read the holy Bhagavata Purana, the ancient Mahabharata and Ramayana, if one went to satsangs and talked with kind and wise swamis about God and the world – just like others had done here centuries ago.

So much of what was written in pious periodicals now sounded odd, much that had formerly vexed him mightily he now found ridiculous, much of what others believed they had to fight for seemed unimportant.

Not that he had been superficial formerly, but only now did he discover the reality of his own inner self – the real reality. He learnt to understand what the gurus designate as 'maya', the unreality of all that is not eternal. The unreality of so many pious and patriotic phrases, the unreality of so many establishments, the unreality of so many claims.

And he discovered that the actual debate took place here, that this reality did not have a smooth, lacquered surface but that it was in motion – struggling. That he had to expect mental struggles not even suspected formerly, that he began to understand increasingly what he had read often, that our struggle is not against flesh and blood, but against the forces and powers in the air . . .

One has to be 'clever', of course. Nobody commits himself, nobody endangers himself, nobody tells the truth. Each one speaks in patterns and passwords of the day, and thinks himself courageous if he utters an opinion that is not accepted by all. Each one thinks of himself, of his prestige, of his money. . . . The truth must be suffered. Truth challenges. One has to surrender to truth – truth is like a gigantic wheel which, once set into motion, crushes anyone who does not follow the movement. Strangely enough, truth is never agreeable. And he found the challenge of truth within himself to be the essence of the encounter. He never attacked anyone; but the battle was there. He gained nothing from the many learned books the school theologians had written at a safe distance to show their erudition. Dialogue was different – completely different.

Dialogue was not a mere talking about religion; that is very often pure babble, vanity, self-glorification. Nor was dialogue the 'comparative religion' of experts. The comparison of religions is interesting only so long as one has not understood what religion is really all about. One can only compare what lies on the surface – maya. The real dialogue takes place in an ultimate, personal depth; it does not have to be a talking about religion. But something does distinguish real dialogue: the challenge. Dialogue challenges both partners, takes them out of the security of their own prisons their philosophy and theology have built for them, confronts them with reality, with truth: a truth that cannot be carried home black on white, a truth that cannot be left to gather dust in libraries, a truth that demands all. Truth was there in so many a true dialogue; never before had he felt so small, so helpless, so inadequate. All of a sudden the shallowness of all religious routine was laid bare, the compromise with the world, that which is essentially un-Christian in so many things that bear Christ's name. Suddenly he became aware of the fact that he, too, had to be 'converted', that he could not confront his neighbour as one who demands, but that they both jointly would have to ask God for his grace. If dialogue is taken seriously, Christianity must be deeply sincere and upright – different from what it is now. He understood that the lack of 'conversion' of the nations was not due to their obduracy but to the lack of conversion among those who had sent themselves. He understood the danger of surrounding the Church with walls and contemplating only what was within these walls, of regarding the small subtleties of those who are 'in' as integral parts of God's salvation plan, of regarding the political opinions of church people as revelation. . . . Dialogue in depth shatters the self-confidence of those who regard themselves as guardians of the whole and only truth. Truth has to be searched for in order to be had; the kingdom of God is arriving, and only those who are on their way will reach it.

How strangely empty and flat those books now seem to us, those books that have been written on other people's religions as though they were museum pieces, or like a grammatical exercise. How little they understand of Christ who believe him to be bound by rules and views of men who want to imprison him in a dungeon of formulas and prohibitions! How surprisingly Christ revealed himself in so many a talk, in so many a struggle – and how very much alive his adversary proved to be as well, he for whom the theoreticians of the dialogue have but a smile, if they do not forget him altogether! How little the dialogue depends on our philosophical systems – and how personal is all that is done by God! How deeply we experience within the dialogue how God loves every man, cares for every man, guides every man! And how aware one gets, within the dialogue, of man's sin – the forgetting of God, the resistance to his guidance, the hate . . .

How little does human theology know – it occupies itself with ideas and words, not with the WORD! So much of what has been written on the 'salvation of non-believers' sounds arrogant; much that is said about the theory: 'Without the church no salvation' is so very un-Christian. What a monster we have made of God . . .

For our theologian, dialogue was not a tactical move for winning church members that could not be won by other methods. Dialogue was, for him, the presence of Christ, the life of the church, his vocation. Before he could speak he had to listen – to God, who also spoke to him through the partner in the dialogue.

This listening was much, much more difficult than he had imagined. The partner had thought more deeply, possessed greater knowledge, a much more subtle way of thinking, an age-old culture and tradition – and of all this he had to learn much in order to understand. And he understood that learning can be a very real form of love, that without this form of love, talking had been but an empty ringing, giving had been tactics, the self-consuming had been nothing. No psychological tricks were necessary, no rhetorical fusses – but substance, honesty, searching, depth, respect for other people's freedom, seriousness in effort.

He had believed all this to be self-evident for those who had been trying for many years to spread the gospel. It was not self-evident. For most of them it was foolishness, impractical, a waste of time . . .

But he was not alone. Men who had had similar experiences, men who had understood that the kingdom of God is within, met almost by chance. A handful, a small group . . . but enough to give one another support.

These people did not form a sect – they belonged to different groups of the church. Many still struggled for Christ; many could not bring themselves to join an organized church, even if in their hearts they believed and had been baptized.

They met endeavouring to find Christ in India's holy scriptures, in the encounter with the people of the country, in the Bible. And it was ONE Christ, ONE Lord of all. . . . Not the small Christ of the sects, but the great Christ who enlightens every man in this world. Christ who is grace and judgment for the person he encounters.

'Blessed are the poor . . . blessed are those who suffer persecution. . . .' He was not spared the bitterness of the beatitudes. No one is spared them, who takes Christ seriously. He read the gospels with completely new eyes. He did not need form criticism or demythologizing. Life itself was the surest demythologization – not a life in a theological laboratory, but in the reality of this myth that lived here. We demythologize because we know nothing – we believe our ignorance to be everything . . .

A theologian friend enquired anxiously how things stood with the faith after such a long time in non-Christian surroundings. . . . What did this man mean by faith? His bookish wisdom? Was faith not more than that?

Formerly, it had scandalized him that Gandhi had called his own life 'an experiment with God'. As if one could experiment with God! The theologian friend would have found his 'experiment with faith' equally scandalizing. It is not possible to experiment with faith. God 'experiments' with us. Our faith challenges us to risk this faith. As long as we are not ready to stake our own nearness to Christ for our brethren we do not know the meaning of faith. Unless we have reached the very bottom of our nothingness we do not know who Christ is.

10

'What do men say about the Son of man?'

The most devout among the Hindus call him an 'incarnation' – one of Vishnu's avataras such as Rama, Krishna or Chaitanya. Others venerate him as the great teacher of righteousness, as a saint whose selflessness and spirit of sacrifice are a model to men. Others again consider him to be a great miracle-worker, like the yogis in ancient times, or like Ramakrishna or Sai Baba nowadays. In many a Hindu home and even in many a temple there is a picture of Jesus – mostly a picture of the Sacred Heart of Jesus, of Italian origin – and many a guru illustrates his upadesha, his religious instruction, with parables from the New Testament and with incidents taken from the lives of Christian saints.

And what do we tell the Hindus about Christ? That they had misunderstood him, that they did not accept his uniqueness which we insist upon, that they denied that without him there could be no salvation.

They have understood exactly what we told them: we told them he was the 'Son of God'. The expression is familiar to Hindus – even before there was a Christendom, epics about 'sons of God' were known in India – Bhima, Arjuna, dozens of heroes descended from Shiva, Brahma or Vishnu – each of them is a 'son of God'. And for the majority of Hindus, for the followers of Advaita Vedanta, God is a provisional quantity – there are as many 'gods' as there are creations, countless ones. A 'Christ, Son of God' belongs to creation. Many discussions, misunderstandings, paradoxes and deliberations matured into a few insights – they make me suspect where the Indian problem of Christ lies, where India meets Christ.

I understand that a literal translation of the gospels and of christological dogma would not lead anyone who had grown up in the Indian tradition to Christ. The gospels presuppose the religion of Israel, and the christological dogmas presuppose Greek philosophy and its problems.

The main concern of India is 'brahmavidya': knowledge of the supreme, union with the Absolute. Gods are temporal – theologies are but constructions that assist in creating the preconditions for an all-embracing experience. Does not Christ's concern also lie on this level? 'That they may know you, Father, and him whom you have sent.' Christ brought no new theology, no new theory of God. He did not even bring 'revelation' in a formulated sense – he *is* the revelation of God. But he is not visible to those devoid of spiritual eyes, nor audible to those with only natural ears. 'God is spirit' – 'The Lord Jesus is the spirit'. For the present, India does not require any new dogmas on the nature and person of Christ – India seeks the Christ experience in depth: the experience of reality. Dogmas become necessary when false dogmas have been formulated. Not before that. Only grace can give salvation. Grace from the living, real Christ, who is much greater than all human comprehension. To 'know' of Christ signifies so much more, in the language of the scriptures, than to apply the categories of Greek metaphysics to some aspects of the phenomenon of Christ. Christ is no philosophical problem – Christ is the mystery of salvation.

Christ can do without the categories of Greek philosophy –

Christ issues from the depth of godhead, he is the One through whom and in whom and for whom everything was created. Including India. Including the Indian mind. India is seeking Christ if it seeks Brahman – it does not seek Western theology.

One begins to understand the relativity and narrow-mindedness of Western theology only after delving deeply into another kind of theology and thereby gaining surprising new insights. And there, too, one discovers Christ.

The great religions never start off with a proof for the existence of God. They presuppose it as the only absolutely assured truth. The existence and reality of other things have to be proved, not the existence of God. Religion begins with existential experience. Categories come later – they touch but the general, the abstract, the past. The pre-abstract, concrete, existential and present experience is dependent on an 'attitude'. If the right attitude is present, the right experience follows. Existential experience is irrevocable – it becomes part of the nature of man.

What is this 'fundamental Christian attitude'? This is part of the problem of the Indian Christ, because it is necessary for the experience of the mystery of Christ. 'First seek the kingdom of God and his justice . . .' The 'kingdom of God' was the great passion of Christ – Christ never 'explains' it. He calls; he claims his property. He does not discuss, he proclaims it – in parables, so that they may 'hear yet not understand'. This appeal from person to person, the answer being the 'imitation', brings about the transformation of man – the real 'conversion'. The more I learnt of Hinduism, the more surprised I grew that our theology does not offer anything essentially new to the Hindu – that even some of the problems had really been treated much more subtly and circumstantially by Hindu scholastics than by our Christian ones. And yet – even if we should discover that the gospels do not say anything 'new' either in content or theologically, the 'vocation' of the Christian would be as meaningful – absolutely new and original on the existential level – as God-experience. In many respects this experience is the exact opposite of Vedantic realization of Brahman. And this is the starting point: for the proclamation of Christ in India we do not need Greek philosophy nor Western science. We must render audible the 'call' of Christ within the words and structures of Indian thought.

The 'search for the kingdom of God' is in itself already 'grace', identical with Paul's 'faith' and John's 'love'. It is the awakening of the latent Logos in every man, the realization of the search for God inherent in man – it is the manifestation of Christ himself as the movement 'towards God' in every being. Its formulation and mode of expression depend on given cultural and historical conditions. The expressions used in the New Testament pre-suppose the Old Testament; Western Christian theology pre-supposed Greek philosophy. Christ himself only presupposes 'his own'.

There are many schools and sects within Hinduism. In order to explain to a Hindu the meaning of 'seeking the kingdom of God', we must enter into his sphere of thought. 'Ram Rajya' is the literal translation of kingdom of God – its meaning is monopolized, in India, by a fanatical political Hindu party. A political 'kingdom of God' – not the kingdom of God Christ died for.

When we transpose the knowledge of Christ into the depth of Brahmavidya, we begin to understand that, essentially, the stipulations set down by Indian theologians for the attainment of Brahmavidya are a first step towards knowledge of Christ: Christ who is not one of many story-tellers, but a Christ who is Logos of God. For Shankara, the Advaita theologian, these are the preconditions for attainment of Brahmavidya:

distinction between reality and illusion, renunciation of all worldly pleasure, self-discipline and peace and blameless life and the desire for ultimate freedom. Dispassionate renunciation is the highest precondition for the supreme passion after the ultimate 'freedom'. Ramanuja, the Vishishtadvaitin, requires man's total and unconditional surrender to God; this is the precondition that renders us worthy of the grace of God which alone can save.

Once I had understood that, I found a shadow of the mystery everywhere – I read the texts with new eyes, texts which outwardly seemed to prove a doctrine so different from Western Christian theology. But Christ is much greater than our understanding – he does not reveal himself so clumsily and primitively as we often imagine a 'praeparatio evangelica' to be. He needs no falsifications of pious people smuggling the name of Christ into pre-Christian scriptures, he was with humanity from its inception, he knows all tongues and guides all hearts, he has many names unknown to us.

What name does he have in India? The giving of names, the shaping of categories and forming of notions is one of the principal occupations of the human mind. In the names man 'understands' reality – he confronts the world as knower. Just as the religions are distinguished from one another by their pre-supposed basic attitudes, so they are distinguished by their basic categories.

In this sphere of distinction, teaching and learning are possible – it is the sphere of genuine theology. It helps man to clarify basic insights, to test, to compare.

John determines the essence of logos as '*prós-tón-theón*' – Christ is present where there is 'movement towards God'. No other category seems adequate for him: Christ is not 'good' or 'holy' or 'great' in the sense these words usually convey. He himself always makes use of a basic distinction: 'My Father' on the one side – everything else on the other side. This basic distinction is truly 'Christian': he judges men and situations, not on the basis of other people's judgment or according to so-called objective criteria, but in their relation to the Father. From this position he judges everything, also institutional religion. In order to go the way of Christ one has to 'know God'.

A large section of Hindu tradition regards 'viveka' (distinction between eternal and temporal, real and unreal, Brahman and maya) as an indispensable condition for Brahmavidya. Our Western philosophy, translated literally into Hindu terms, relegates Christ into the sphere of the noneternal, of maya, of the temporary. Our narrow moral Christian understanding of 'good' as opposed to 'bad' compels Hindus to range it under dvandvas, the finite pairs of opposites within karma.

We have to clarify that the 'Christian' distinction is as radical as the one between Brahman and maya: that Christ belongs in the sphere of Brahman. Without this radical distinction, religion would be meaningless and its demands on man purely poetic exaggerations of unjustified encroachments. Knowledge of Christ takes place inside Brahmavidya – not in the cognition of temporal things.

Another insight had been won – an insight of far-reaching importance: Christ does not come to India as a stranger, he comes into his own. Christ comes to India not from Europe, but directly from the Father.

It will never be possible to contain Christ's mystery and the essence of Christianity completely and adequately in terms and ideas. It is only because, to us, certain terms have a Christian meaning from earliest childhood that we believe something like 'Christian terminology' to exist, – expressing Christ exclusively and directly. If we start to ponder over the terms used by Greek christologists and think them out to their logical extremes, then we fall into absurdities and heresies. The first christologists were so aware of the newness of Christ and of the inadequacy of all known terms, that they preferred to talk about Christ paradoxically. The paradox denies and asserts both terms that exclude each other. A seeming contradiction, it is, however, the only means that compels our thinking to excel itself. The statement that 'logos' had become flesh is equally directed against a spiritualistic and a materialistic misunderstanding of reality. Christ is neither the incarnation of the Jewish idea of God nor the apotheosis of the Greek idea of man. In India, too, we will have to make use of paradoxes, in order to lay open the mystery of Christ: the paradox evokes an existential cognition because it compels man to surpass the purely terminal, to advance into the essence, into the one reality where no contradiction subsists. I tried for myself to go through the various 'margas' developed by Hinduism and to test them for their 'cognition of Christ'. The result was, for me, surprising in more than one respect: I found that I could learn from the Indian savants' insights to understand Christ in a new way; I found there, already developed, what I thought I had to begin.

Much of what Indian tradition had to say on the subject of the 'word' was a wonderfully profound illustration of what John says of the 'word' in his gospel. Every finite word we utter is sharing in the eternal, uncreated, original word, a word that is brought forth perpetually by Brahman, Brahman himself in the shape of the word. 'Brahman, without beginning or end, the indestructible essence of the word, manifest in the shape of things, the source of creation . . .' – one of Bhartihari's sayings. The subject of 'sacrifice' as treated by the karmamarga theologians, offers many essential insights and often surprising parallels to the theology as expounded in the Epistle to the Hebrews. A Vedic hymn describes how Purusha, the original god-man, is sacrificed and how from this sacrifice everything visible and invisible is created.

A good deal of misunderstanding about Christ and his sacrifice could be avoided if we did not translate literally the Hebrew imagery and terms but made use of India's tradition: not in order to stop there, but to continue: 'This is a symbol for the present time. . . .' Christianity is a religion of love – a 'Christbhakti', the Hindus call it. In the centre of the Christian bhakti stands Jesus – as Krishna is the centre of Krishnabhakti and Rama is the centre of the bhakti as practised by the devotees of Rama. Christ is not identical with Krishna and Rama – the Hindus, too, know that.

The scope of bhakti is not speculative. The God of the bhaktas is a God become part of human history – their puranas are not a collection of legends and myths, but redemptive history – description of the redemptive activity of God in his various advents. The Puranas treat of the great themes of every history of redemption: creation, dynasties of God's people, biographies of saints, practical wisdom and rules for the moral and cultural life. If we ignore the teachings and themes of the Puranas and simply give the Hindu a literal translation of our Bible, we but enlarge the misunderstanding that Christianity is one of many bhakti sects, Christ one of many avatars, the Bible one of many puranas. The fables and myths of the puranas have a deeper meaning – their Christ-meaning. Bhakti has a very subtle terminology, a widely ramified theology. I began to understand how little those preachers who had made use of bhakti terminology actually understood of the connections and background.

The theological problem of Christ in India has always appeared to be that India does not wish to recognize the uniqueness and exclusiveness of the saviour Jesus Christ and has always harped on the fact that there were many saviours – that Krishna and Rama and all the other avataras stood on a same level with Christ. The great scandal of Chrisian preachers! They themselves were the cause. They introduced Christ as an 'avatara' – the 'only' and 'exclusive' avatara. And this, for a Hindu, is sheer nonsense – a limitation of the freedom of God who adopts any form when and where he pleases. In Indian theology there must be many avataras. If Christ is an avatara, he cannot be the only one!

Is Christ an avatara? Even an elementary knowledge of bhakti theology will show at once that the Church's understanding of Christ would exclude the use of a term like avatara. If only the missionaries did not always consider studies a superfluous waste of time. . . .

Bhakti theology does have a category for Christ – for the uniqueness and exclusiveness of Christ: in Pancaratra theology of the fivefold manifestation of God there is an 'issue' from the supreme Brahman, expressing very well the essence of Christ – and his uniqueness. Even the other manifestations can be understood as sacramental presence, as inherence, as spirit. . . Many details of this theology are a revelation of the 'unknown' Christ; much of it leads us, too, towards a better understanding of Christ.

In the theological college we had spent a lot of time refuting pantheism: one of its most important varieties was, of course, Vedanta, especially in the form of Advaita. Already at that time I felt that the professor of theology who treated this subject did not know much – if anything at all – of Indian philosophy in general and of Vedanta in particular. Later, when reading Meister Eckhart – which is now permitted even in seminaries – I began to understand how so-called 'pantheism' has a much deeper insight than a tame academic theology that wants to prove everything and always puts the theses right at the beginning of the lecture, to make absolutely sure that the result will be correct.

I found Vedanta extremely attractive and I believe that, in Advaita, essential human insights are expressed. When speaking with Christian priests in India, it was apparent that they either had not the slightest idea of Vedanta – or did not know what to make of it: 'Vedanta, but that is pantheism, refer to Denzinger number so and so. . . .'

In Advaita Vedanta, the difference between Brahman and non-Brahman and the identity of atman and Brahman are absolutely established. The sphere of sensual perception is complete in itself – the sphere of Brahmavidya is absolutely transcendental. Brahman cannot be recognized through inference of causality ('proof of the existence of God') nor through perception, but only through identity. Only Brahman can recognize Brahman. This realization requires complete detachment from all things finite. Brahman is not even remotely 'like' something else – Brahman is only like Brahman.

Hindus with an Advaita background often asked me whether there was no esoteric Christian tradition; surely the gospels, treating only of things in the sphere of karma, the highest of which is a heaven, could not possibly be all there is. John denies explicitly the existence of esoteric teaching by Christ; he has said everything there is to be said, he has described the true Christ.

John himself presented the 'adhyatma Christ' – if one knows how to read his gospel. The New Testament, too, knows the basic differentiation between the variable and the invariable, between illusion and reality, between sense perception and faith, between flesh and spirit. Christ himself, according to John, meant his miracles to be 'signs' – maya. . . . Even the apostles begin to understand that, in the night preceding his death, he speaks 'openly and no more in parables', when he reveals to them the mystery of union with the Father. This is adhyatma cognition of Christ: 'I am in the Father, and the Father is in me . . . I in my Father and you in me and I in you. . . .' The karma reality of whatever can be seen and heard by means of the senses is a 'veiling' of reality, illusion, maya. The seeing of an unspiritual man is non-seeing, his hearing is non-hearing, his faith is self-delusion. Paul constantly stresses the reality of Christ as being a spiritual reality – kyrios is pneuma! The Lord Jesus is the spirit! The centre of the Christian message is a reality of the spirit. The radical character of the Christian detachment from the world is as total as the detachment of an advaitin from karma. Jesus says that, 'without him, we can do nothing'. Paul says that 'our true self is Christ, not we'. Only Logos can have full knowledge of God; to know Christ requires a complete emptying. That is precisely what we have to lay stress on in our message: the cognition of Christ is of the nature of Brahmavidya; Christ is not one of the puranic sons of God, who are many and limited. Christ is unique in the same sense as Brahman is unique – has to be unique, not in the sense of one among the avataras who may claim pre-eminence. Knowledge of Christ requires no less spirituality than Brahmavidya. To become a Christian does not imply an outward application of 'remedies', but a deeply spiritual 'realization'. Christ is not outside Brahman in the province of karma, but in the very 'heart of Brahman', 'in the cavity of the heart'. Therefore, the way to know Christ is through realization of the inner life . . .

I have not finished yet. Not for a long time. I know there are many closed gates to pass before the knowledge of Christ becomes full reality. But I believe this is the way. Christ is not an idea, Christ is not an emotion, Christ is not a religious museum-piece – Christ is the Logos of God: in the encounter with Hinduism I have begun to understand how Christ meets the Hindu – not from the outside, but within his own thought and faith.

When I mentioned some thoughts of this kind to a professor of theology, he declined: 'If we say it in this way, the Hindus will reply: Why then your Christianity, if we already have Christ in our own religion?'

When I mentioned the same thought to Hindus, they confessed to have understood the meaning of Christ for the first time – that they knew now of the newness of Christianity, that they knew the claim of Christ, that they now understood.

My experience is that, commonly, the Hindus themselves say something quite different from what people who think they know Hinduism through bookish learning expect them to say. Most Christians, brought up in a Christian tradition and culture and never removed from Christian surroundings, have lost a sense of what differentiates Christianity from non-Christian religions. That which is essentially Christian surely does not lie in a certain formulation of enunciations on God.

I asked myself whether we did not render Christ very doubtful service by simplifying his message – when we make of him a teller of stories, a moralizing schoolmaster, a less-than-serious dreamer. By remaining on the surface of an outward religiosity, do we really preach Christ?

Greek christology has not exhausted the mystery of Christ, though it has helped the Church the better to see some aspects of Christ. Indian wisdom, too, will not exhaust the mystery of Christ. But it would help the Church in India to understand Christ better and to let him be really understood: the knowing of Christ as the revelation of the mystery of Brahmavidya – Christ, the desire of the eternal hills . . .